Weekend Millionaire® Real Estate FAQ

Weekend
Millionaire®
Real Estate FAQ

MIKE SUMMEY
ROGER DAWSON

McGraw-Hill

New York   Chicago   San Francisco   Lisbon   London
Madrid   Mexico City   Milan   New Delhi   San Juan
Seoul   Singapore   Sydney   Toronto

The McGraw·Hill Companies

1 2 3 4 5 6 7 8 9 0   DOC/DOC   0 9 8 7 6

ISBN 0-07-146307-0

While we have tried to make everything is this book accurate, please be aware that all 50 states have different real estate laws and those laws are constantly changing. Even legal interpretations of those laws change constantly. We cannot guarantee the accuracy or completeness of the information in this book. For your own protection, you should consult with local real estate professionals, attorneys, and CPAs before making decisions based on the information in this book.

McGraw-Hill books are available at special quantity discounts to use as premiums and sales promotions, or for use in corporate training programs. For more information, please write to the Director of Special Sales, Professional Publishing, McGraw-Hill, Two Penn Plaza, New York, NY 10121-2298. Or contact your local bookstore.

 This book is printed on recycled, acid-free paper containing a minimum of 50% recycled, de-inked fiber.

Contents

Contents

Contents

Weekend Millionaire® Real Estate FAQ

PART I

Principles of Real Estate Investing

This part consists of five chapters devoted to defining the basic principles of real estate investing. There are dozens of real estate gurus traveling the country giving advice on how to get rich quick and quit your job. We understand that building wealth is not about how big your house is, how expensive a car you drive, or how fancy the clothes are that you wear. Wealth is not the standard of living you live but how long can you sustain that lifestyle if you suddenly can't work and earn. Since our best-selling book *The Weekend Millionaire's Secrets to Investing in Real Estate* (McGraw-Hill, 2003) was published, we have received thousands of questions from our readers, some from e-mails, some from our Web site chats, and many from the call-in radio shows on which we have been invited to appear. The chapters that follow mirror the chapters in that book and consist of a compilation of questions and answers pertinent to each chapter. This book is designed to be a companion for our real estate book and to act as a resource that answers your questions about long-term real estate investing.

Place this book side by side with our real estate book. As you read and questions pop into your mind, just flip to the corresponding section of this book, and probably you will find your questions already answered in this book. If you don't find the answer here, the bonus section at the end of this book will show you how to use our Web site weekendmillionaire.com to communicate directly with us and get answers live and in real time during our scheduled chats.

Whether you read this book through from beginning to end or just use is as a backup resource while studying *The Weekend Millionaire's Secrets to Investing in Real Estate*, we're sure that you will find it informative and helpful in your real estate investing career.

1

Get Rich Slowly

The first thing you need to understand about *The Weekend Millionaire's Secrets to Investing in Real Estate* is that it takes more than just one weekend to become wealthy. In fact, while it is an investing strategy that can be done on the weekends, it requires investing a little time each weekend and doing it regularly for many years. Throughout your life, you invest a little of the income you earn from your job into Social Security or any of several other retirement plans with the hope of being able to retire around age 65. But for those of you wise enough to devote a little of your spare time to investing in real estate the way we teach, you may be able to retire many years earlier, as Mike did at age 50.

The questions that follow came from our readers and relate to the concept of getting rich slowly.

Jobs stink! How long should I have to wait before I quit my regular job and go into real estate investing full time?

Principles of Real Estate Investing

Jobs may stink, but they pay the daily bills while you're building wealth. If you're looking for a magic bullet that will get you to instant wealth—try the lottery. Wealth building is a slow process; however, the lack of job security is all the more reason to get started building a real estate portfolio. Unless you have a sizable sum of cash to invest and great credit, it may take years before you can build a large enough passive income stream to enable you to completely quit working and just live off your real estate. One thing you should think about: Your job may stink, but it sure beats no job, which is the alternative until you are generating enough cash to live off your investments.

Many people talk about all the money they are making flipping or rehabbing properties. The Weekend Millionaire philosophy seems to advocate buying and holding only. Why don't you recommend flipping, rehabbing, or other lucrative techniques such as subject-to, lease options, short sales for foreclosures, etc.?

The Weekend Millionaire philosophy is an investment philosophy. The other money-making techniques you describe are just money-making techniques. When you flip a property, or rehab and resell a property, it hopefully produces a lump-sum profit, but the deal is over. You no longer have your investment out there working for you, which means you traded today's labor for today's profit. You have to find another one of those deals to make another profit. The other techniques you mention such as subject-to, lease options, and short sales of foreclosures are buying techniques that can fit well with the Weekend Millionaire philosophy, which is to invest today's time and money into deals that will pay you for the rest of your life.

I am just getting started, and I've signed a contract for a house that needs repairs. Should I keep it as a rental after I get it fixed up, or should I sell it and make a profit that I can use to buy more properties?

If the contract you signed followed the guidelines from *The Weekend Millionaire's Secrets to Investing in Real Estate,* you should be able to fix it up and rent it without having to consider selling it. Granted, a quick profit looks good, but wealth building is a slow process, not a get-rich-quick scheme. When you acquire properties that will rent for enough to cover the expenses and pay off the loan, tenants are making monthly deposits into your future each time they pay the rent. Mike took no money out of his real estate for over 20 years. When he finally did start taking money out, he was in a position to take out enough to retire with a very tidy sum each month and to do so at age 50. Just remember, wealth building requires patience.

Why do you recommend not selling any of your properties?

We feel that when you buy good income-producing properties and let them produce income over time, it is a surer and more secure way to wealth. When you sell, you cap your profit at the time of the sale. By holding properties and allowing inflation to push rents up and the passage of time to pay off the mortgages, the margin of profit becomes increasingly wider over time.

Even with 30-year variable-rate interest-only loans, it is hard to make deals that generate cash flow. As the property values continue to increase, isn't it going to become impossible to buy properties that will make money?

It's hard to make any property show a positive cash flow in the beginning. This is why the Weekend Millionaire method is not a get-rich-quick scheme. Cash flow comes as the rents increase and the mortgages pay down over time. If you can buy properties that just break even in the beginning, eventually the cash flow will become a trickle, then a stream, and finally a torrent as inflation pushes up rents and mortgages are paid off.

Do you ever worry about the market turning down and vacancies increasing, which could lead to financial distress for investors? Isn't that a greater risk when an investor is highly leveraged?

Periods of extremely low interest rates enable many people who have been habitual renters to buy homes. Vacancies increase because of this, and investors who are overleveraged and do not have cash reserves experience some difficulties. Fortunately, the low rates also enable investors to refinance their loans and improve their cash flows. The low rates also produce a strong sellers' market, so those who are unable to refinance often find buyers ready to take the properties off their hands.

So the key is to make sure that you have plenty of cash on hand just in case, right?

That's one of the things we advocate in *The Weekend Millionaire's Secrets to Investing in Real Estate.* Start building cash reserves right from the beginning. Even if it's just a few dollars each month, be sure to set aside reserves to tide you over during slow times or when major expenses arise. As in building wealth in general, building cash reserves is a slow process, but it is well worth the effort both to protect your assets and to build better banking relationships. The key to getting rich in real estate is leverage. You want to own as much property as you can with as little of your own money as possible, but that doesn't mean that you should keep all your cash invested. You're far better off to finance 100 percent of a purchase and keep your cash in the bank than you are to put 20 percent down and finance 80 percent. The cash you tie up in down payments can't be used to carry you through slow times or to cover unexpected expenses. As one of our students said, "I must say Mike is true to his word when it comes to his belief that this is a get-rich-slow scheme. When I told him I bought four properties this year, he told me to hold off buying any more until I built up some cash reserves."

Your book talks about buying one property a year to put you on your way to financial freedom. You also talk about being patient. Do you think it's wise to keep waiting for everything to line up in the rest of your life before making a move, or do you think that sometimes you just have to take the plunge and make things happen?

We recommend taking the plunge, but we also recommend looking first to see if there's water in the pool and if you're diving into the deep end. The first few properties you buy still will feel like you're taking a big risk. Once you gain some experience, you will feel more confident. As you learn the business, you'll understand that you're really not taking big risks. The antidote to fear is education, but education without action is paralysis.

What's a good amount to have on hand before buying your first property?

Once you start looking and making offers, you will find that there are properties you can buy with little or no money down. This doesn't mean that they are good deals, but they are out there. Once you buy your first property, we recommend that you try to keep enough cash on hand to cover three months' expenses with no income. This may seem like a lot, but if you will allow your profits to accumulate in the bank rather than pulling them out for something else, you can accumulate this reserve faster than you think. If you're just starting, try to build up some cash reserves before you make your first purchase. By doing so, you will avoid getting into trouble if the property is vacant for a month or two or if you have an unexpected large expense.

Most people have made so much money on their personal residence recently that it is tempting to consider moving up to a larger home. Although your home isn't really an investment per se, the amount of leverage you can get with a low down payment and good owner-occupied interest rates makes it very enticing. What do you think?

The money most people have made on their personal residences is only paper profit. Even though values have gone up, unless you sell or refinance your home, the profit is all on paper. If you have a great deal of equity in your home, you'd be better off obtaining a home-equity line of credit and using the funds to purchase investment properties than buying a bigger residence. Investment properties produce additional income, whereas a bigger home takes a larger bite out of your earned income.

I am in the middle of a rehab right now and hopefully will rent it out next month. I want to keep looking for more, but my wife is a bit leery. She wants me to wait six months before buying another property. I was going to lease option it, but after reading your book, I decided to keep it. Should I keep looking or take my wife's advice and wait?

Keep looking, just for the experience, but it wouldn't hurt to take your wife's advice before making another purchase. Getting some experience as a landlord helps, but if you can find a real steal in the meantime, we wouldn't discourage you from buying it. Just be sure that the deal is an exceptionally good one.

If you have the money "lying around," wouldn't you be better off paying cash for a property? Even if you only earn 6 to 8 percent on the investment, isn't that better than getting 1 to 2 percent from a bank?

Yes, earning 6 to 8 percent is better than 1 to 2 percent, but leverage is the key to building wealth with real estate. For example, if you have $100,000 in the bank, and you use it to pay cash to buy one house that cost $100,000, you could easily earn 6 to 8 percent on your money, but you would only gain appreciation on the one house. On the other hand, if you used your $100,000 as down payment money and bought five to ten $100,000 houses, your tenants would pay off the mortgages, and you would gain appreciation on $500,000 to $1 million worth of real estate. As mortgages pay down and values go up, rents rise and cash flow grows.

Everyone in my real estate club says, "Use a hard money lender, and don't use your cash." What do you think?

See the answer to the preceding question. In addition to using leverage whenever possible, holding onto your cash gives you the added advantage of having cash reserves. Maintaining good cash reserves makes you far more attractive to lenders than the amount of equity you have in real estate.

Even if we have the cash on hand to buy another property and pay for it in full, do you still think that we should save the money and keep it as reserve funds? Where will we get the seed money to buy another property?

We don't advocate that you never put any of your cash into a purchase. We simply want you to take it slowly and never put yourself into a position where unexpected expenses or vacancies can cause you to lose your properties. A good rule of thumb is to pace your purchases so that money generated from your current investments provides the seed money to buy additional ones. We know that this may seem like a very slow pace in the beginning, but it will keep you moving forward and keep you out of trouble. Let appreciation grow the value of your properties, let your tenants pay your mortgages, and if necessary, refinance and pull out part of the equity to buy another property. In the meantime, if you hang onto your cash, you will have a healthy reserve in case of emergencies. Lenders like that, and you will too.

It seems that Mike has acquired many properties. At what pace did he buy houses when he first started?

Mike bought his first investment property in 1972, but he didn't buy another one until 1979. He then bought two in 1980, four in 1981, and gradually increased his numbers as his expertise and cash flow grew. He did just what we are recommending; he took it slow and steady, and as a result, he has never had to sell a property.

I've listened to your CD audio program and have finished your book. They are great companions that work so well together that I can't understand why everyone doesn't have them. I've already told my brother about them, as well as many of the people I work with, but could you tell me what makes your program different from all the other real estate programs I see advertised that seem to promise overnight wealth?

There are a lot of people out there selling get-rich-quick real estate schemes. Personally, we've never found one that works over the long term or that creates wealth as we define it. Sure, there are ways you can turn a fast buck with real estate, but most of these are speculating rather than investing. Like the lottery, everyone wants to talk about the winners, but no one mentions the millions of losers. We prefer a steady, secure approach to wealth building over risky speculating.

I must admit, I've been watching real estate infomercials on TV since I was in college (20 years ago). When I read your book, I was amazed at how sensible it was. There are no outrageous claims or unrealistic expectations, and everything is based on sound analysis, and that is what interested me. What is your opinion of all those other real estate programs?

We have bought and still buy the materials produced by other real estate gurus. You're right when you say that some of them contain outlandish claims and unrealistic expectations, but our philosophy is that if we can pick up just one idea that helps close a deal, it's worth the cost of the program.

Often it's like looking for the proverbial needle in a haystack, but we've yet to read or listen to another real estate program from which we didn't learn something.

I've always wanted to pursue real estate and have decided that now is the time. The problem is that I'm not quite sure which way to go. I have about $170,000 cash, a log cabin in Vermont worth about $30,000, but absolutely no income. I know that your program is a get-rich-slowly plan, but is there a way to generate income from the start? I read the section about the value of owning a property free and clear and thought that if I buy one property for cash, I could take out a loan against the equity and look for more rentals. I have found a few duplexes and thought I might live on one side and rent the other. Do you think this is the way to go?

There are many ways to generate quick income from real estate, but we're not the best ones to ask about it. There are people who make money by buying, fixing up, and flipping properties. Others make money by locating super deals, getting them under contract, and then selling the contract to investors; still others do quite well buying and selling real estate notes. To generate quick income, you just about have to rely on one of those methods. Generating income this way is not investing; it's speculating. It's buying with the hope of selling quickly for a profit. Our experience is with buying and holding properties to generate passive income. This is a long-term strategy in which income is very small or nonexistent in the beginning, but as the mortgages pay down and inflation pushes rents up, the cash flow grows. This is not a strategy for someone with no income unless he or she is already independently wealthy. This strategy works well if you are employed with an income to cover your daily living expenses. You can then treat your real estate investments like a 401(k) plan or an individual retirement account (IRA) and let them grow and mature.

2

Wealth Is an Income Stream

Wealth isn't what you own, nor is it the lifestyle you live; many people have gone broke living high on the hog and owning stuff. The true measure of wealth is the size of the income stream from your investments . . . in other words, the money for which you don't have to work. Many people trade labor for money and then use that money to live a grand lifestyle, but often these people are just a paycheck or two away from financial disaster.

Here's a group of questions we received that deal with wealth building.

Is now a good time to be buying houses? It seems like it is very hard to find any good deals.

Any time is a good time to buy if you buy right—the way we teach you in *The Weekend Millionaire's Secrets to Investing in Real Estate*. Granted, there are times when finding good deals are easier than at other times. During periods of very low interest rates and a strong economy, there are more buyers in the market, and this can make finding good deals harder—but not impossible. To build an income stream, which is the true measure of wealth, you must be patient and wait until you find the right deals. By doing so, you will be able to withstand the ups and downs of the market that kill others who buy expecting to sell later at a profit and do so without considering the cost of owning the property until they get it sold.

Can't you build wealth by flipping houses instead of working a job?

You can make money flipping houses, but making money and building wealth are two different things. All the work that goes into finding properties you can put under contract at prices that will allow you to flip the deals to investors or other buyers is like having a full-time job. Yes, you frequently can make a few thousand dollars on each deal, but it's not a steady income. A good job gives you a steady income on which to live and allows you the freedom to look for investment properties that you can acquire for the income they can produce. If you treat them like you would a 401(k) and just let the mortgages pay down and the value increase, you will build significant wealth over time.

So if flipping houses is a business or a job, then buying and keeping rental properties is building an investment portfolio, right?

That's right! There are many ways to make money with real estate—buying, selling, brokering, developing, flipping, rehabbing, etc.—but there's only one way to build wealth as we define it. Buy to hold and build an income stream. It's the stream of passive income that ultimately will secure your future and allow you to quit working . . . if that's what you really want to do. All those other ways of making money in real estate require you to keep working in order to keep the money coming.

How much equity do you recommend taking out of a particular property to use to buy more properties?

After you build up equity in one property, you can refinance it to get cash to invest in additional properties, but you shouldn't think of it as pulling out equity. When you reinvest the money into another property, you are merely rolling equity from one property to another. In the end, when the deal is done, you still have the same amount of equity; it's just spread out over more properties. We recommend that you do this as often as possible without putting yourself in a position where you are overleveraged. We want to caution you about this because property values have been increasing faster than rents for the past several years. In many cases, this has made it possible to borrow more on a refinance than the rental income will support. As you approach the time when you want to retire, you may want to slow down and let the equity build up so that you can increase your stream of income more rapidly.

If we follow the Weekend Millionaire program, does it mean that we may have to be 20 years into the program before we can quit our jobs? What would we have to do to retire earlier?

From the beginning we have stressed that the Weekend Millionaire program is not a get-rich-quick scheme, but this doesn't necessarily mean that it will take 20 years either. However, even if it did, what's wrong with taking 20 years to retire if you can do so with many times the money you would have otherwise? Unless, of course, you are already near retirement age. The number of years it takes to be able to quit your job is directly related to the amount of time and effort you put into it. If you invest the time and energy to locate and purchase several properties a year, you will get there faster than someone who is content to just buy one property a year.

What is the preferred method of getting equity out of a property you already own? A home-equity line of credit (HELOC)? Create a note?

First, we don't want you to think of it as getting equity out. If you take the equity out of your real estate investments, you lose much of the compounding effect that generates wealth. Building more equity translates into building a larger income stream. The stream of income you generate is your true measure of wealth. Now, with that said, we feel that a line of credit secured by equity is the most flexible and probably the best way to use equity to purchase additional properties. The more properties you own, the more tenants you have paying off mortgages, the more value you have appreciating, and the faster you can build wealth.

Principles of Real Estate Investing

*How much capital does it take to get started? I'm new to real estate invest-
ing, but I have a lot of friends who are flipping properties to gain some capital first. Is this a good way to start?*

If it would make you feel better to flip a few properties to build up some
working capital, by all means do so, but you can still make offers that will
work with the money you have. Don't spend a lot of time worrying about
what you don't have. In the beginning, most investors don't have a lot of capital. What's most important is that you make offers that will work for you in
your current situation. So many new investors lack the patience to wait
until they find deals that really work, so they pay too much or structure the
offers wrong and end up in financial trouble.

*Once you acquire a large number of properties, what happens if you
have a large portion of your tenants who give notice at the same time?
Wouldn't this severely cut into your cash flow and cause financial worry?*

If you suddenly lose a large portion of your income stream, it would cause
concern. This is one of the reasons why we recommend that new investors
start small with single-family homes rather than apartment buildings. We
also recommend that no more than 20 percent of your properties be in
close proximity to each other. About the only way there would be a sudden
mass exodus of tenants would be due to some outside factor making the
properties or the area suddenly undesirable—something like the discovery
of toxic waste buried on or near the property, the construction of a noisy or
smelly industry nearby, etc. If your properties are small and scattered in the
beginning, it gives you added protection from sudden income loss. Even
after you get started, we still don't recommend that you get overly invested
in one property or one area.

*I currently own two properties with about $80,000 equity between the two.
There is enough equity that I could refinance one of the properties and pay
off the other. How can I use this equity to purchase more property?*

If you refinance one of the properties for enough to pay off the other one,
that will leave you with one property free and clear. When you find another

property of similar value to the one that is free and clear, you can borrow against it to obtain the money to offer cash for the new purchase. In real estate, investors say that "cash is king." You often can get the best deals when you can make cash offers. When you borrow against a property you already own, you usually can get a higher-percentage loan than if you apply for a new loan to purchase a property.

Since you define wealth as an income stream, is it a good idea to offer to lease option your property rather than just to rent to a tenant? Couldn't you get a higher monthly income, and isn't it true that few purchase options are ever exercised?

We don't like lease options because we don't like it if the options are exercised. Yes, you usually can get a little higher rate, but you also risk losing the property. We don't see much advantage for you to lease option properties you already own, but it can be a great tool to use when you are buying, especially if you don't have much cash to put down. You lease option the property and then rent it out to a tenant to cover expenses. If it goes up in value, you exercise the option; if it doesn't, you can renegotiate. Yes, it's true that few lessees end up exercising their options, but if the property has gone up in value, it's more likely that they will—and you lose the equity gain that could have been yours.

How can you get started building an income steam when you don't have money for the down payment on properties?

When we started, we didn't have money for down payments either, so we had to find deals that we could put together with little or no money down, and it wasn't until we had several properties generating cash flow that we could wait for enough funds to build up in our real estate accounts to make another deal. This meant that it was slow going in the beginning because finding deals that would generate cash flow with no money down was difficult back then, just as it is now. However, it's not impossible. Being patient and looking until you find the right deal is not all bad. It tends to slow you down and allows you to get experience writing offers and learning more about how to evaluate properties.

What about investing in a 401(k) if you are in the corporate world? Is this a good idea, and if you are already in one, would you cash out and put the money in real estate?

When Roger left the corporate world, he cashed out every penny from the profit-sharing plan he'd been paying into for 13 years, took the money, and tripled it in real estate in six months. Retirement plans are long-term investments, and so is investing in real estate the way we teach in *The Weekend Millionaire's Secrets to Investing in Real Estate*. If you follow the advice in that book, you should be able to do far better than you could in a 401(k) plan. However, we don't recommend that you pull your money out and put it into speculative real estate ventures. Buying and holding real estate for the income stream it produces is investing. Buying real estate to resell for a profit is speculating.

Is it realistic to have a goal of making $30,000 per month positive cash flow within a year, and if so, what would be a good plan to do it?

Having a goal of $30,000 per month positive cash flow is realistic, but unless you have a tremendous amount of cash to invest, doing so within a year is not. Having that much positive cash flow probably would require you to own 20 to 40 fully paid-for houses. While the goal is realistic, the time frame is not. It takes time to find and purchase properties, especially when you're looking for wholesale deals. If you can pay cash for the properties, you will reach the goal much quicker, but if you're like most people and finance the purchases, it takes the cash flow longer to build up while you (or should we say your tenants) are paying down the mortgages. Having a goal like that is key, but set a realistic time frame and don't allow setbacks to discourage you. Just keep at it little by little, and you'll get there.

I wanted to get into flipping properties, owner financing, and lease options to generate money more quickly. In the meantime, I could let the rents continue to grow for the properties I want to keep long term. I know the Weekend Millionaire approach is to hold and not sell, but doesn't selling accelerate money coming in?

Yes, selling can accelerate money coming in, but it also caps your profits at the time of sale. You will never make any more money from the properties you sell. If you sell for a quick profit and then reinvest the profits into more properties, you may be okay, but most people take the profits and have a good time with them. You have to keep your investments compounding, and you don't do that by selling. Look at the example on page 4 of our real estate book, which shows you how to reach a million dollars by doubling a dollar 20 times. You will notice that $786,432 of that million is reached with the last two doubles.

If all your mortgages are paying off principal, does that mean that your tenants are buying the properties for you?

Absolutely! This is what makes real estate investments such wealth-building tools. Anytime you can get someone else to contribute to your retirement account, that's money you don't have to earn to put in yourself.

I'm a beginning investor. Is it advisable for me to form a limited liability corporation (LLC) to hold title to the properties I purchase, or should I just purchase them in my own name?

Titling properties in an LLC may add some measure of liability protection, but in our opinion, LLCs are better used for estate planning purposes. Even if you title your properties in the name of an LLC, you probably still will have to personally guarantee the loans until the LLC has enough assets to be a good credit risk by itself.

You recommend sending your bankers monthly statements. Do these statements include only the loans for their banks, or does it include your entire portfolio of real estate loans?

We recommend sending your bankers a statement that shows your entire portfolio of properties, including those with loans at other banks, as well as those with no mortgage at all. The purpose of this statement is to keep all your bankers apprised of how you are doing overall with your properties. In order to build strong banking relations, you have to keep your bankers informed in such a way that they feel comfortable with your ability to perform on any loans they might make.

My goal is to build wealth with rental properties. I have a few. My main question is, should I sell a property that is in my Roth individual retirement account (IRA) that has no debt and has been rehabbed? It would put me in a better cash position, or should I tough it out and hold it for the income stream?

You need to make that decision based on your personal circumstances, but just keep in mind that if you sell it, you cap your profits at the time of the sale. If you hold it, it can continue to earn for the rest of your life. Owning an income property that has no debt is like having a goose that lays golden eggs. Why would you want to sell it? A third option would be for you to borrow against it and use the money to buy more properties, thus increasing your leverage power.

If I have cash to invest, am I better off buying 2 or 3 homes for cash, or would I be better off using my money to make down payments on 10 to 15 homes and put mortgages on them for the balance of the purchase price?

In most cases you are better off buying several homes, putting mortgages on them, and then letting the tenants buy them for you. This is how you use leverage to build wealth, especially if you have a few years left before retirement. However, if you are already retired and need the income your cash can generate, then you may be better off with fewer homes in order to have money on which to live and also have less risk.

As our income grows, how do we reduce the risk of being sued? In today's age of litigation, we're concerned about being sued by one of our renters and losing what we've built up over the years in some frivolous lawsuit.

Liability concerns are one of the reasons we recommend using professional property managers. We require the management companies to carry both liability and errors and omissions insurance. This provides a buffer between us and the tenants. You may want to consider holding your properties in limited liability corporations (LLCs) as an added layer of protection. Since the names of the LLCs can be totally different from your name and the address of record is often a post office box, practically none of your tenants will know who you are or how to contact you. With all that said, the best lawsuit protection is being a good landlord who doesn't create hazardous situations in and around your properties.

3

Income-to-Value Ratios

Understanding the relationship between value and price is critical to success in real estate investing. The combination of what you pay and how you pay it is what determines value. In the United States, where people are seldom taught anything about negotiating terms, price is the sole factor many people use to determine whether or not an investment property is a good buy. When you buy with the intention of holding properties long term, does price really matter as long as the income produced by the property will pay off the purchase price in a reasonable time? We don't think it does, but this concept is difficult for many people to understand.

Here are some questions our readers have posed to us about price, value, and terms.

I have just signed a contract to purchase a property, and I will use my home-equity line of credit (HELOC) to pay cash for it in the amount of $29,000 at prime rate and to rehab it at an additional cost of approximately $15,000. Is this a good plan—to buy the $29,000 property for cash *and get 100 percent cash flow and then to use it to secure a line of credit to purchase additional properties using this same approach?*

This is a very good plan, especially since the $29,000 property should appraise for much more once you finish the rehab and get it rented. You may want to wait a few months before you attempt to get a line of credit using it as collateral. Not only will this result in some equity buildup, but it also will allow the deal to "season" a bit before you apply for the loan. Banks like this because it lets them see that you can manage an investment property properly. The only flaw with your plan is that you won't actually get 100 percent cash flow because even if you are planning to pay the payments on your HELOC out of other income, it still affects your overall cash flow.

What percentage of rents should I allocate for maintenance, management, vacancy, etc.?

The maintenance percentage will vary from property to property depending on the condition of the structure. Naturally, you will not need to allocate as much for a new house as you will for an older one, especially one in which "big ticket" items such as the roof or the heating and air-conditioning systems are approaching the end of their useful life. We call this "deferred maintenance." You will have to reserve a much larger percentage for maintenance if you are going to have to replace these items in 2 to 4 years rather than 15 to 20 years. The cost of management should run from 4 to 12 percent of the rent depending on the area, your ability to negotiate with prospective management companies, and the number of properties you have to manage. Vacancy percentage will vary from area to area and with market conditions. A good property manager can give you the best advice on the numbers for your area.

Do you recommend 15- or 30-year mortgages?

We recommend that you use the shortest-term mortgage you can make work with the net operating income (NOI) the property will produce. This could be a 20- or 25-year loan instead of a 15- or 30-year. Some real estate gurus recommend long-term loans to produce better cash flow in the beginning. We favor the delayed-gratification approach, which is why we like to see our properties paid off as quickly as possible. Granted, the cash flow is not as good in the beginning with a 15-year mortgage as it would be with a 30-year loan, but we know that the best cash flow comes when there is no mortgage, and we like to get to that point as quickly as possible.

Considering the fact that it is easier to qualify for adjustable-rate mortgages (ARMs), would you recommend these, or should we stick with fixed rates?

It all depends! During a period of high interest rates, when you are relatively sure that rates will be trending downward, the ARM may be a better deal. On the other hand, during periods of very low interest rates, getting an ARM may put you in a position where you can't make the payments if the rate adjusts upward significantly. You should lock in low fixed rates when they are available. Another option and one we frequently use is a fixed-payment/adjustable-rate loan. With this type loan, the payment is usually fixed at an amount based on ½ to 1½ percentage points above the going rate, and then as the rates move up and down, the payment remains constant. This type of loan and the fixed-rate loan make cash-flow planning an easier task.

This may be a dumb question, but what's the difference between percentage interest and points on a loan?

Percentage interest is the rate of interest you pay on the outstanding balance of a loan until it is paid. Points are fees charged in the beginning when a loan is first established. One point equals 1 percent of the loan amount. Points typically are fees paid to lenders in exchange for lower interest rates on loans.

How do closing costs figure into the equation when you are trying to determine what to pay for a property?

You should estimate closing costs and consider them as part of the purchase price when you make an offer. They have to be paid at closing, just as the purchase price does, and like depreciation, they are expensed over the life of the loan.

Do you recommend using a home-equity line of credit (HELOC) as a way to get started investing in real estate?

For many people, the only real asset they have is equity in their home. In the absence of cash, a HELOC can be a valuable tool that allows you to use this asset in lieu of cash to make investment purchases. Just be sure to factor the payment you will have to make on the HELOC into your calculations when determining what to offer for a property. HELOCs can be wonderful tools if used correctly. They can provide the seed money you need to put deals together that you usually can refinance in a year or so for enough to repay the HELOC. This can give you a source of funds to keep making more and more deals.

Is there a percentage of market price you won't go above, or do you always base it on making the numbers work? As long as you can cover your costs, does price really matter?

Keep in mind as you read this answer that we are talking about buying properties to hold to build long-term cash flow, not properties to turn for a quick profit. With this thought in mind, even if you can buy properties at 50 percent of market prices, you can still go broke if they won't generate cash flow. On the other hand, if you could find a way to pay 50 percent above market price and have a positive cash flow, you'd be successful. In *The Weekend Millionaire's Secrets to Investing in Real Estate,* we show you how to calculate the value of a property without having to worry about appraisals, listing prices, or market prices. If the numbers work, the price is irrelevant; if they don't, it's not a good investment regardless of the price.

When you say "if the numbers work . . . ," do you mean "show a positive cash flow"?

That's correct. We recommend that you don't buy unless you can have at least breakeven cash flow.

So does that mean that you sometimes go over market price when you can make the numbers work?

Real estate is a long-term investment; therefore, price is only part of the equation. To determine the value of real estate investments, you must consider both price and terms (what you pay and how you pay it). Yes, you can pay an above-market price if the terms are significantly below market rates. This is where the income-to-value relationship comes into play. When you obtain financing from sources whose business it is to lend money (banks, etc.), you aren't likely to get below-market rates, but many sellers are willing to provide such financing if they can get their asking price. As a long-term investor who plans to hold properties to build an income stream, virtually any deal you can structure that will allow you purchase properties with the net operating income (NOI) is usually a good deal.

4

Small Rent Increases Snowball Your Net Worth

An amazing phenomenon that real estate investors experience is the effect of small rent increases on net worth over time. Since investment properties usually are financed over long periods of time using loans that have fixed payment amounts, each small rent increase widens the gap between monthly income and cash going out. This gap between income and expenses is called *cash flow* and is what most investors monitor on an ongoing basis.

While the focus is on cash flow, what is often overlooked is the increase in value of investment properties as rents rise and cash flow improves. This increasing value widens the gap between what is owed on the property and what it is worth. This gap is called "equity," and since net worth is defined as the difference between what you own and what you owe, the equity growth resulting from rising rents causes net worth to snowball over time. This is one of the reasons we are strong advocates of the buy-and-hold strategy of real estate investing. We don't turn fast cash like some people who rehab or flip properties, but we do build a growing stream of passive income and the accompanying substantial net worth that enabled us to retire early and not have to worry constantly about how to make another deal.

Here are questions we have received about our strategy.

If you refinance when interests are higher, won't your payments go up, and how will this affect your net worth?

When you refinance, you usually do so to pull part of your equity out to use for other things. This doesn't always mean that your payments will go up; they may well go down because you're extending the years over which you'll pay off the loan. However, it does mean that your equity in that particular property will go down. Let's assume that you bought a property for $100,000 and borrowed $80,000 when you made the purchase. If over time the value of the property increases to $150,000 and the loan pays down to $40,000, you still will be making a payment that was originally based on an $80,000 loan. If you refinanced, even at a higher rate, but only took $20,000 of the equity out of the property, your new loan would be $60,000, and the payment could be less than what you were paying on the $40,000 balance of the original loan. In this scenario, your payment could go down, but your equity also would go down. Instead of $110,000 equity, you would have only $90,000. If you refinanced back to the 80 percent loan-to-value position you were in when you originally purchased the property, your new loan would be $120,000, your equity would drop to $30,000, and your payment probably would be substantially higher than it was before. If you kept up with inflation by having small annual rent increases, you might be able to refinance to the higher amount and still have the property generate cash flow. If you keep the cash in the bank or reinvest it as equity in other properties, you net worth will not go down; however, if you use the money for a vacation, a new car, or some other purchase that goes down in value, it will negatively affect your net worth.

How do adjustable-rate loans affect cash flow and net worth?

If you have adjustable-rate loans, you're vulnerable during periods of rising interest rates. Small rent increases that keep up with inflation help to make the higher payments that come with rising rates, but adjustable-rate loans during periods of rising rates do have a negative effect on cash flow. This also has a negative effect on net worth because when rates rise and payments increase, more of your money is going to pay interest and less to pay off the loan. This results in slower equity buildup and/or reduced cash flow. We always advise people who use adjustable-rate mortgages to build up cash reserves adequate to cover any shortfall that may result from increased payments.

What are your thoughts on trying to raise rents when tenants are already paying at or above market rents?

If your rents are currently at market value, you run the risk of losing tenants if you try to go above market rates without giving them something in return. Market rates are influenced by many things other than just inflation. If everything stays the same, inflation will justify small rent increases annually, but very low interest rates, economic downturns, overbuilding, loss of jobs, and other factors also affect rents. These are all factors you need to consider when making investments.

What is the best way to gauge rental rates? I watch the newspaper ads, but are there other good sources for determining rental rates?

One good way is to do some competitive shopping by acting like a renter and finding out what choices are available in your town. Look for "For Rent" signs, check with property management companies, check ads in local weekly or monthly shopper's guides, and look for real estate publications that are often found in "Free" racks scattered around town. You'll quickly get a feel for market rental values. Your best source of information on market rates is your property manager. This is his or her business.

The real estate agents whom I talk with discourage me from buying and holding properties to rent. They point out that I can make as much profit now by selling as I would if I held the properties for several years. Why shouldn't I follow their advice?

Probably the biggest reason the real estate agents try to encourage you to sell is because that's how they make money. A secondary reason may be that they don't understand the difference between investing and speculating. They are correct when they tell you that you often can make as much profit on a sale as you would on several years of renting. What they don't tell you is that when you sell, you cap your profit at the time of the sale and never make another dime on those properties. When you buy and hold, profits start out as a trickle and gradually build to a torrent over time as mortgages pay off and rents increase. The beauty of this strategy is that the longer you own the property, the wider the margins become, assuming that you keep the property well maintained. It's a slower process, but it lasts a lifetime and allows you to keep adding to your income year after year.

Is it the small rent increases or just inflation that increases property values?

The way small rent increases build net worth is by increasing the net operating income (NOI) of your properties. Yes, inflation increases value, but rent increases support this value increase. Even without inflation, a higher NOI still would equate to an increase in value. The more income your properties produce, the more they are worth. For example, a property producing a $1,000 per month NOI would give an investor $12,000 per year or a 10 percent return on a property valued at $120,000. If the NOI is increased to $1,300 per month, or $15,600 per year, this would give the same 10 percent rate of return on a property valued at $156,000. When dealing with single-family homes, market demand may push values up faster than the NOI increase would warrant, but this is usually due to demand from homeowners wanting to live in the properties. In cases such as this, should the demand dwindle, prices may fall—but never below the price that investors will pay for the income stream.

5

What Makes a Property a Good Buy?

Becoming a successful real estate investor is not a lot different from running a successful shoe store. If you are going to be in the shoe business, you can't pay retail for your shoes and then sell them for retail and stay in business. Being a successful investor is no different: You can't pay market value for your properties and then rent them for market value and stay in business. There has to be a margin of profit. This is why we stress the importance of buying properties wholesale. Is this easy to do? No! Is it possible? Very possible, but as with anything worth having, you have to work at it. Unfortunately, most people want to arrive at the destination of financial independence without taking the journey. This is probably what makes lotteries so popular—the lure of a huge payoff for very little investment. The problem is that for every million-dollar lottery winner, there are millions of one-dollar losers. Real estate is not like this. You can assure yourself of becoming financially independent by following a few common-sense principles, and one of these is to properly evaluate what makes a property a good buy.

What Makes a Property a Good Buy?

Here are some of the questions that readers have asked about this concept.

I found a four-unit building in the Los Angeles area. How do I valuate the property to see if it is a good buy?

First, follow the steps in *The Weekend Millionaire's Secrets to Investing in Real Estate* pertaining to computation of net operating income (NOI). Then see if you can structure an offer that will allow you to purchase it with the NOI. If you can do this, you will have a good deal.

I just bought a house and found out that it appraised for $30,000 more than I paid for it. Would you consider this a good deal?

Don't get hung up on appraisals. They are for banks and people who want to feel good about buying a home in which to live. We have seen many properties that could be purchased far below appraised value that still were not good deals for long-term investors. Buying below appraised value and then hoping to make improvements and sell for a higher price is a totally different strategy from buying to hold for long-term income. We call this "speculating," not investing. As they say in Vegas, you are "betting on the come." With this approach, sometimes you win and sometimes you lose. The Weekend Millionaire strategy is to buy right, hold for rental, and then let the passage of time make you rich.

Is it okay to just break even on a deal? In other words, is any deal that can be structured to at least break even, based on the initial net operating income (NOI), a good deal?

We think so. If you do your calculations properly and consider factors such as deferred maintenance into the equation, any purchase you can make that will allow you to buy with the NOI should turn out to be a good deal. If you at least break even in the beginning, as the mortgage pays down and the rents go up, the margin of profit will rise. Remember, becoming wealthy requires three things: patience, patience, and patience!

I have an opportunity to get an existing property on which the current owner makes about $100 a month. He has offered to sell it to me, but the deal he has offered would require me to subsidize the property by about $50 *to $75 per month. Wouldn't this be a good deal because rents are rising, and it would only be a year or two until I am in a breakeven position?*

Our rule for all markets is: If the numbers work, buy it, but if the numbers don't work, don't buy it. The logic behind this is that we want you to be in a position that if the market softens and rents don't rise the way you anticipate, you can still avoid negative cash flow. Mike once bought nine properties from an investor who had done just that. After more than four years of negative cash flows that had exhausted all his savings, the investor ended up selling the properties at a huge loss just prior to their being foreclosed on. Just remember: *No one ever went broke because of the property they didn't buy.* Thousands of people have lost fortunes on properties they bought wrong.

We are seeing a lot of U.S. Department of Housing and Urban Development (HUD) foreclosures coming on the market in our area. Are these usually good buys?

Once again, run the numbers. If you can buy them with the calculated net operating income (NOI), by all means do so. If you can't, treat them like any other potential purchase and pass them by. If you want to know more about HUD listings, you can check out what's available in your area on the HUD Web site at www.HUD.gov. However, we want to caution you about www.HUD.com; it's a foreclosure service and not the official government Web site.

Regarding U.S. Department of Housing and Urban Development (HUD) foreclosures, does the government have any guidelines on how much discount it can give off the list price?

The government receives advice from local brokers on how to price properties, but its primary interest is providing loan guarantees, not owning property. For this reason, it wants to get the properties off its books as quickly as possible. This doesn't necessarily mean that it will offer the properties at fire-sale prices. During strong seller markets, you can expect to find very little in the way of discounts. The longer a property remains unsold, the more incentive there is to keep discounting the price until it sells. There are special brokers who take classes to become qualified as HUD brokers. These brokers typically list the HUD homes and handle their sales.

What Makes a Property a Good Buy?

How does the length of a loan affect whether or not a purchase is a good buy? Is there any advantage to using 15-year loans versus 30-year loans?

Naturally, the longer the loan, the lower is the payment, which helps to keep it within the available cash flow, but age has a lot to do with it also. If you're in your twenties or thirties, a 30-year loan isn't that bad if you want to get your properties paid for before you retire, but by the time you reach your fifties, you tend to want to get them paid off as soon as possible. Our recommendation is to always use the shortest-term loan you can make work with the available net operating income (NOI). We've actually made purchases that we were able to finance for just 10 years.

Wouldn't it always be better to always use 30-year loans so that you could have more cash in the beginning to reinvest in other properties?

In theory, the answer to this question would be yes, but this assumes that you actually would accumulate the extra cash and reinvest it. Our experience has shown that most people use the extra cash to raise their standard of living now rather than reinvesting it for the future. We believe that shorter loans act like forced savings plans that make you invest the extra cash by paying off the loans and build net worth faster. Very few people have the discipline to set aside the extra $50 to $100 each and every month until they can find another property in which to invest.

How do repairs factor into whether or not a property is a good deal? I've found two possible investment properties. One needs only a few hundred dollars' worth of work, but the other needs at least $10,000 worth of work to make it ready to rent.

The amount of work needed to put a property in rentable condition is not important if you allow for it in the purchase offer. When you calculate the net operating income (NOI) you expect a property to produce and are trying to figure out how much to offer, you first have to reduce the NOI by the amount of return you want on any down payment you make plus the money you will have to spend on repairs and then structure the offer based on the remaining NOI. Unless you do this, you may overlook the fact that you should get a return on the cash you put into a deal, whether it is in the form of a down payment or repair costs.

Maybe I'm just impatient, but it seems that the price of property is so high in relation to the rent you can get for it that it is nearly impossible to find a good investment property. Is now a good time to buy, or should I wait?

When trying to make the numbers work, keep in mind that there are only a limited number of properties that can be purchased wholesale. Your challenge as an investor is to locate these properties. We've been investing for over 30 years, and we've heard this same concern expressed the entire time we've been investing. This is why you have to keep making offers. You should expect to have most of your offers turned down, and you shouldn't become discouraged by these rejections. Remember, true wealth building is not a get-rich-quick proposition. Compare spending a few hours each week looking at properties and making offers with what you do on your job. If you're like most people, you work 40 hours a week, 50 weeks a year, for 40 years and end up with little more to show for it than the meager retirement Social Security provides. If it takes you an entire year of making offers to buy your first property and buy it right, within 15 or so years, that one property easily could pay you more than the Social Security check for which you worked your entire life. Imagine the effect that spending just four hours a week and only buying one property a year could have on your life if you did it consistently for 15 years.

Is there a simple rule of thumb that I can use to compare sales price versus rental price to tell quickly if a property is a good deal?

Some people advocate using a gross rent multiplier to determine value. This is a multiple of the annual rent that often ranges from 7 to 14 times the annual rent. Another variation is a multiple of the monthly rent, often ranging from 80 to 130 times the monthly rent. We don't place a lot of stock in "rule of thumb" gross rent multipliers because they don't take into consideration financing terms, condition of the properties, rental demands, market conditions, and other factors that you are forced to consider when you calculate net operating income (NOI) and then use it to determine if you can buy the property.

PART II

Learning Your Real Estate Market

Beginning investors are nearly always nervous about taking that first step toward purchasing investment properties. This is a natural phenomenon and nothing to fear. Even seasoned investors like Mike and Roger get butterflies when stepping out of their comfort zones to consider investments that are outside their level of experience. However, as we stress in our book *Weekend Millionaire Mindset* (McGraw-Hill, 2005), growing requires stretching and getting out of your comfort zone. Part of this growing process is learning the market in which you plan to invest.

This part of *The Weekend Millionaire's Secrets to Investing in Real Estate* explores topics that range from finding property managers, selecting areas on which to focus your attention, the Threshold Theory, types of properties with which to get started, and dealing with asking prices. The chapters that follow in this part provide answers to the many questions readers have posed on these topics. We realize that no matter how hard we try, we won't cover everything, so as you read, remember that if questions come to mind for which you can't find the answer in this book, you can always go to our Web site weekendmillionaire.com and ask the questions in the live investor chats that we host as a *free* service for our readers.

If you will register as a "New User" when you visit the Web site, you will receive e-mail notices letting you know when these chats will be held. We don't want anyone to give up on their investing dreams because they encountered an obstacle or situation they didn't know how to handle. The purpose of this book and the live chats is to provide the resources you need in these times.

Now let's move on and explore some of the questions we've received on the subjects contained in this part.

6

Finding a Property Manager

The issue of finding a property manager seems to produce several concerns for new investors. These range from issues of trust to questions about why one would want to pay part of their income for someone else to collect the rent. The first thing that you need to address is whether you want to be a landlord or an investor. Being a landlord takes a lot of time and involves legal issues, liabilities, and headaches. There are professionals who keep abreast of the legal issues, market conditions, and other factors that must be considered when dealing with renters. These people also have a stable of repair people available who can handle almost any repair that needs to be done. We recommend using a property manager from the very beginning of your investing career. Not only does it put a buffer between you and the tenants, but it also frees up your time to look for good deals on additional properties to purchase.

The following questions address many of these concerns and should help you to become more comfortable with using a professional property manager and to better understand why we make this recommendation.

Learning Your Real Estate Market

You recommend hiring a management company even for the first property. When you have only one property, will a property management company even talk with you, let alone give you a good rate?

Good management companies realize that tenants are much easier to find than owners. If they are trying to build their companies, each new property becomes a potential profit center for them, so yes, they will talk with you when you only have one property. You won't get as good a rate with one property as you can negotiate when you have several, but you should get a fair rate. If a management firm tries to charge small investors too much, word will get around, and it will hurt them in the long run. In most markets, you should be able to find good management for around 10 percent of rent collected.

For those of us who are landlords, how much handy work should we try to do after we have dozens of properties?

This question is easy to answer: None. The highest and best use of your time is looking for more properties to buy. Don't manage your own properties. You should get someone who specializes in property management to do both the management and the maintenance so that you can focus on finding more deals.

My wife doesn't think that I can succeed because I am not a handy person at all. I'm having a hard time convincing her that I don't need to be a handyman to be an investor. What can I do to convince her?

Have her read our books, and show her the answer to the preceding question.

It is so cool that you are so successful without having to deal with all the mess I'm dealing with. I have one guy who isn't paying his rent, so I guess I'm going to have to evict him. When do you recommend starting the eviction process? What is the last straw?

Professional property managers keep up with the laws in the states where they operate, so they know how to evict tenants the correct way and not get sued. This is another reason why we recommend professional management. As for when to start the process, we recommend starting the first day possible under your state laws. Our property managers know to do this with all our properties. Past experience has taught us to not tolerate past-due rents and not to delay starting the eviction process because the tenants have problems. Delaying the start simply allows the tenants to shift their problems to their landlord. Since the process takes from several days to several weeks, the tenants have that long to correct their problems and bring their rent current. If they can't do this, you are on track to get rid of them at the earliest possible date. Sure, they may have to pay the cost of the eviction papers to stop the process, but that's their problem, not yours. They created it, not you. This may seem harsh, but when you establish rules for your tenants and enforce them to the letter, you end up with better tenants.

Since you are big on using property managers, how do you avoid getting burned? How do you protect yourself from property managers who overpay for repairs or simply charge for repairs that aren't done?

Lesson one in using property managers is that they do what you "inspect," not what you "expect." As an investor, instead of using your time to manage the properties, you focus on managing the managers. Give them strict limits on what they can do without your permission. Review the monthly reports you should receive on the properties, and if you question a charge, ask to see the work that was done. In most states, property managers are required to be licensed, and part of the licensing process is being honest in the handling of owners' funds. Mismanaging clients' funds is grounds for license revocation in nearly every state.

How do you select a good manager? Do they have property managers associations you can go to for information?

NARPM is one national organization, and there are other associations both state and local. But the best way is through personal interviews with several in your area in order to find one with which you have a good rapport. Do a Google search, and then check the Yellow Pages and classified newspaper ads. Then discuss what you expect and what they expect, and make sure that you are in agreement.

Don't you run into problems with management companies, such as not following up as they should on vacancies, etc.?

Properties managers are like any other employees; they have to be managed. This is the reason we say that you should conduct an in-depth interview with a management firm before you hire it. Make sure that you are in agreement on how vacancies, repairs, and other duties will be handled, and then insist on it being done. Random inspections keep managers on their toes. If you allow them to slack off on their duties, they probably will do so unless you have an exceptionally good one.

I recently interviewed a property manager who wanted a "finder's fee" of 75 percent of the first month's rent when he secured a tenant. Is this normal? What do you think?

It all depends. Is this a full-service management firm or merely someone who is being contracted only to find a tenant? If it is a full-service management company, we think that you should find another one! A full-service company is going to receive an ongoing percentage of the rent, which should be adequate compensation.

I passed on a pretty good opportunity last week because I learned that the property manager I was planning to use wasn't totally honest (I discovered that he wrote some bad checks and took some money for properties that weren't available). Do you think that this was the right decision, considering that the property had a nice net operating income (NOI) and should have given me a healthy cash flow?

Don't let good deals pass by because you don't have a property manager. It will take several days to close, and you can use that time to find one. You can always take care of things yourself for a few days rather than miss a good deal. You were right to run from a manager with a reputation for dishonesty. Never give a person like that a second chance.

When you're getting started, shouldn't you plan to do as much of the work as possible yourself? I know you don't recommend this, but until you can build up some cash reserves, you may have to.

Our opinion is that if you can't afford to pay for management and maintenance, you probably paid too much for the property. If you do decide to do the work yourself, just be careful that it doesn't use up all your valuable time.

Finding a Property Manager

In other words, don't spend $100 per hour time doing $10 per hour work. Look for a handy person whom you can trust. This can do wonders for you. Pay him or her by the hour, but make it clear that you only pay for the time he or she is working and not for time spent running to the store to buy something he or she forgot.

Do you have any tips on identifying good property managers?

We recommend that you write down all the things you want a property manager to do for you, and then, when you interview prospective candidates, use your notes to address all the issues. Listen carefully to the responses you receive, and then use your best judgment to select the one that impresses you the most. It works just like hiring an employee after studying the résumés of several and conducting preemployment interviews. The better your interviewing skills, the better manager you will hire.

You say stick to properties close to where you live, but if you have a great property manager you know you can trust, is it okay to invest in out-of-town properties?

Theoretically, you should be fine, but what if something happens to that manager? Can you find another one you trust as much? In some areas you don't have much choice but to invest further away from where you live, but it's always a lot more comfortable to be able to drive by your properties on a regular basis to see how they are doing.

Do you recommend letting the property management companies pay your loans, or would you do that yourself?

It is critically important to handle the payment of mortgage payments, taxes, and insurance correctly. Late mortgage payments affect your credit, and missed tax and insurance payments can result in loss of insurance or liens being placed on your properties. If the management company is late or misses making a payment, it's still your problem. This is why we recommend that you pay these important things yourself. In this way you know that they are done in a timely manner. This used to be a chore, but with today's methods of paying bills electronically, it only takes a few minutes a month.

Other than mortgages, taxes, and insurance, is it okay to let management companies handle basically everything else?

Yes, within reason! It's fine to allow the management companies to handle everything else, but have a dollar limit on expenditures that they cannot exceed without your input. They will be dealing with suppliers and repair people, so how they handle them will not affect your credit, but putting a limit on how much work they can order without your permission will alert you to any large repairs or improvements that could result in a contractor's lien being placed on your property if not paid. When a large expenditure is approved, you may want to pay it yourself so that you know it gets done.

Do property managers charge you for the ads they place in the paper, or is that a cost of doing business for them?

Advertising is part of what a professional management firm does to earn its fee. If the firm wants you to pay for the ads, you should look elsewhere. When the firm is paying for the ads, this increases its incentive to keep the properties rented.

Should the utilities be in your name, the management company's name, or the tenant's name?

Unless you are paying the utilities, the bills should not be in your name. If the tenants are responsible for paying them, then the bills should go directly to them. The landlord often pays utilities on some multifamily properties such as apartment buildings, but tenants usually pay all utilities on single-family homes.

When using property managers, do the tenants pay you and then you pay the managers, or do the managers collect the rent and then pay you the balance after they pay the bills and take their cut out of it?

The rent nearly always goes through the property managers. They pay any maintenance or repair bills, deduct their management fee, and then each month send a full report of income and expenses, including any invoices they have paid, along with their check for the money remaining after the expenses.

Finding a Property Manager

Okay, let's cut to the chase on property managers . . . are there any basic qualities I should look for?

There are two fundamentals you want to be sure a property manager has: honesty and reputation.

What do you do if there are no property managers listed in your area?

There may not be any full-time property management firms, but I'll bet there are real estate firms that do both management and sales. This is not the best scenario, since real estate agents spend most of their time listing and selling because it turns a quicker buck for them; however, sometimes this is the best you can do. Until there are enough properties to manage for a property manager to make an adequate living managing them, he or she has to supplement his or her income with sales commissions.

7

The Threshold Theory

The Threshold Theory says that the more thresholds you cross, and the more properties you look at and make offers on, the better your next buy will be. If you look at 100 properties before making your first purchase, we can almost guarantee that it will be a good buy. If you only inspect 30 properties, your chances of getting a good buy are considerably smaller. It's a numbers game.

We would much rather you took six months to buy your first property than have you settle for a lesser deal just because you got impatient. This means that you may wear out a pair of shoes and put a lot of gas in your tank before you buy your first property. Becoming a Weekend Millionaire takes patience and a great deal of perseverance.

How do you find properties to buy that will be profitable? A friend of mine looked at 35 before he found one that worked.

The Threshold Theory

Mike once made over 50 offers in a row that were rejected, but then when one was accepted, 6 of the next 10 were. It's a numbers game. You just have to keep at it until you find the right deals that work for you.

Would you say that the majority of deals you've made are from people you've met on the street? Just shaking hands and asking for opportunities?

Mike agrees that many have been made that way, but he wouldn't say the majority. Most of Roger's purchases came from real estate agents bringing him deals when he was a broker. You would think that real estate agents would snap up the best deals themselves, but they don't. They make their living from earning commissions, and they need the cash flow that selling properties brings them. Most can only invest a small portion of their commissions, and many can't even do that.

Should we wait until prices come down because right now it's very hard to find properties with positive net operating income (NOI)?

Don't wait for prices to come down. Ignore asking prices, and make offers that work for you. We've bought properties before at 50 to 70 percent of the asking prices. You have to be willing to ask before you can find out what a seller actually will do. You won't catch any fish unless you put a hook in the water.

What were your most effective ways of finding deals, especially when you were just starting?

We just started making offers. Most of them were rejected, but eventually, one was accepted then another and another. We guess that you could say that we stumbled our way to success in the beginning because we did a lot of things then that we wouldn't do now. The longer you're at it, the better you'll get. The key is to not give up when you encounter a little resistance— or even a lot of resistance. Approach it as a game that isn't over until you win.

Learning Your Real Estate Market

How important is it to be familiar with the area where you plan to invest? What's the best way to learn the market?

Knowing the market is critical to your success. The more you know about what's for sale and what properties have sold for, the better you'll be at spotting bargains when you see them. Start by doing research on the Internet to get an overview. Do a Google search for real estate for sale in your town. Or go to Realtor.com, which is the Web site of the National Association of Realtors®. Next, drive around on the weekends and go to every open house you can find. Remember that real estate agents hold open houses to find buyers and sellers, not just to sell the home they are holding open. Let the agents know that you're an investor looking for rental houses. Ask them if they know of any houses that will rent for enough to generate cash flow with a small down payment. Some agents want to work with investors, and some don't. Just keep asking until you find one who wants to be helpful. Call every "For Sale by Owner" in the newspaper, and go see the property. Make it clear to the sellers that you are an investor, not a real estate agent trying to list their property.

I know you have to make offers, but you have to have people calling you. What were your most effective ways to get people to call you about properties for sale? Or did you use a real estate agent via MLS?

We think that cozying up to real estate agents is a great way. Be upfront and tell them that you're looking for rental bargains. Some real estate agents don't believe in buying properties themselves (believe it or not), or they need the cash from the commission more than they need another investment. Running a small ad in the local newspaper also can bring calls. An ad such as, "Need to sell? I buy houses to rent! If you have one you need to sell, call me at XXX-XXXX," can produce surprising results.

Did you ever use direct mail or cold calling? I'm just curious to learn your most effective ways of finding good buys.

We have handed out business cards in a neighborhood, mailed letters and made cold calls to out-of-state owners, and checked public records at the courthouse to find potential sellers. We now use real estate agents most of the time because we have a couple of good ones who keep an eye out for deals for us, but in the beginning, we often simply would take the classified ads and go through them looking for potential deals and then make offers. Do whatever works for you, and don't be shy!

I think that "curb appeal" is an important consideration. When you drive up or drive by a property, does it call out to you?

Curb appeal, which is what a property looks like when you first pull up out front, is important when you're selling or renting property. However, it does tend to push the asking prices up. We suggest that you buy the worst-looking property in the best neighborhood. Mike has several houses in a neighborhood close to his home in Asheville, North Carolina. When he first started buying there, he bought the worst houses in the neighborhood and began to spruce them up. As his properties improved, the other homeowners started to improve theirs. Today, houses that he bought for $30,000 to $40,000 each 10 to 15 years ago are now worth $120,000 to $150,000.

How many offers does it usually take before you can buy a property?

Roger spoke at a convention in Las Vegas recently where some real estate investors were holding a discussion on how many offers you had to make to get one accepted. The consensus was about 30. This is probably true on average, but it doesn't mean that you will have one accepted every time you make 30 offers. Sometimes it may take only 5 to 10, and other times it may take 40 to 50, but the consensus of the investors at the meeting was that about 30 is a good average.

Do you write your own offers or have a real estate agent handle the paperwork?

We've always written our own offers. Only use a real estate agent to write the offer if the property is listed already and a different selling agent has brought the opportunity to you. If you're dealing with the listing agent, you should write your own offer. Mike uses his own contract. It is a cross between the one the real estate agents use and the one that Carleton Sheets offers in his toolkit. He writes the offer, explains it to the agent, and offers to accompany the agent when it is presented to the seller. Since his offers often are unconventional, the agent frequently welcomes Mike's help in presenting the offer to the seller. He always tells the agent that he will present the offer and then leave so that he can discuss it with the seller. Because Roger is a broker, he prefers to use the Association of Realtors approved form. The offer forms that Realtors® use these days are very complicated and are designed primarily to stop the agents from getting sued if something goes wrong.

Do you think that it's an advantage for an investor to get a real estate license?

Mike and Roger disagree on this. Mike says no, and Roger says yes. Here are pros and cons:

In favor of having a real estate license:

- You learn a lot about real estate fundamentals when you study to pass the state test.

In favor of also working in a real estate office:

- You get to see a lot of real estate when you work in a real estate office, so you learn the market quickly and thoroughly.
- You often hear of good buys before they are made available to the public.
- You can use your commission for the down payment. This could be significant if you're low on cash.

Against having a real estate license:

- You expose yourself to liability. As a paid agent, you have a responsibility to do the best you can for the principals. You must inform the buyers and sellers, as well as potential buyers of your property, that you are a licensed agent. Your offers should include the clause: "Buyer is a licensed real estate agent (or broker) buying at below-market value for possible resale at a profit."
- It's harder to look at "For Sale by Owner" property (FSBOs) because the seller will ask you if you're an agent and suspect that you just want to list the property.

Against also working in a real estate office:

- Your selling duties distract you from your goal of buying real estate.

The Threshold Theory

I made an offer on a U.S. Department of Housing and Urban Development (HUD) property and lost by $4,000. It frustrated me because I could have paid $4,000 more and still made it work. Any suggestions?

Well, don't let that discourage you. Keep making offers. We are amazed at the people who will end up paying too much for a property just so that they can say that they bought one rather than being patient and making offers until a good one is accepted. You've heard it said that patience is a virtue. That statement is all the more true in real estate investing.

8

Stick with Bread- and-Butter Properties

What we call "bread-and-butter properties" are single-family homes that will rent in the middle range of rents for a given market. These are typically two- to four-bedroom houses that range from 800 to 1,400 square feet in size. They are basic starter homes—the types of homes to which first-time buyers are attracted. These homes are the most rentable properties you can own, as well as the most liquid real estate assets you will acquire.

Unfortunately, in most markets, the demand for these types of property also makes them the most difficult to find. Their attraction to everyone from the first-time buyer to the most sophisticated real estate investors makes them a hot commodity, which is why they are easy to sell if you need to, especially if you keep them well maintained.

We recommend starting with these properties, and because they are more difficult to locate and purchase at wholesale values, the idea has generated these questions.

Stick with Bread-and-Butter Properties

Any concerns about buying older homes? I live in the Phoenix area, where new and newer homes are selling like crazy and often go for more than the asking price. The only homes I have found that could be bought at wholesale are 30+ years old, and no one wants to touch them. Any reason why I shouldn't?

Our main concerns with older properties are the potential liability that may come from lead paint and asbestos. These products were used commonly in construction prior to the early 1970s. But there are ways to protect your tenants from exposure, even if such hazards exist. Before buying older properties, we recommend that you get a good home inspection and be sure that the inspector checks for those items. If they exist, either you or the seller will need to take corrective actions to mitigate any hazardous exposure.

Is one time of the year any better than another to buy bread-and-butter properties?

Since these homes tend to attract families with children, they generally are more sought after between the end of one school year and the beginning of another. This can produce a larger number of buyers in late spring and early summer. During this time, the competition to purchase can make it harder to find deals than during fall and winter. Remember that with fewer buyers out there, you'll get better buys.

What about the tenants? If there are fewer buyers, won't there be fewer renters also?

This may be true to some degree, but tenants tend to be more transient than buyers. We suggest that you check the classified ads offering houses for rent. Over time, you will get a good feel for how easy it will be to find tenants at different times of the year. Nobody wants to move at Christmas, of course. Also, every market is different, which is why we suggest that you watch the classified ads in your area to get a better feel for the market.

If I had to tell my real estate agent to look for only one type of investment opportunity, what should it be?

If you're just getting started, by all means follow the advice we give you in *The Weekend Millionaire's Secrets to Investing in Real Estate.* Look for conforming neighborhoods where high concentrations of blue-collar workers live. By "blue collar," we mean people who are primarily manual laborers who are likely to be lifelong renters. As your portfolio of these types of properties and your experience grow, you eventually will feel comfortable branching out into small apartments and other types of investment properties. In the beginning, however, stick with bread-and-butter properties.

I'm just starting out and trying to find the best opportunities, but it's almost impossible to find single-family homes that will generate cash flow. What's wrong with starting out with commercial properties if the numbers work?

Let's be sure we're talking the same language. "Commercial properties" are factories, warehouses, and shopping centers, places where the lessee will conduct a business. Apartment homes are called "investment properties." There's nothing wrong with commercial properties if the numbers work. The reason we don't recommend them for beginning investors is because there are so many variables to commercial leases that few new investors have the knowledge and experience required to be successful. One big concern is that tenants are far more difficult to find than with residential single-family homes. It's not uncommon for a commercial property to sit vacant for years between tenants. Few new investors are able to carry a property for extended periods of vacancy without a large cash reserve or healthy positive cash flows from other properties; something few new investors have.

Aren't some houses just too big to rent out? I bought one that is 3,000 square feet with four big bedrooms and three baths. It's huge, and I'm having trouble renting it.

Right, don't buy the big ones. This is one of the 14 biggest mistakes new investors make. Many good deals on large homes are created by people trying to move up socially and getting in over their heads financially. While the deals may look good on larger properties when you compare purchase prices with appraised values, these larger properties generally do not make good rental properties. The numbers of renters who can afford them are few and far between; therefore, vacancies tend to be high. Read about buying "steals" in high-end and low-end properties in Chapter 40 of *The Weekend Million-aire's Secrets to Investing in Real Estate*.

Median home prices in my area are now over $270,000. How can I pay that and make the numbers work when rents will not come close to supporting that kind of price?

First, forget median price; look for deals in basic starter homes, which typically aren't your median-priced houses. Second, when prices seem high, you should focus more on negotiating terms. A $1,000 net operating income (NOI) can cover the payment on a 15-year mortgage in the amount of $100,000 at just under 9 percent interest, but it will cover the payments on a 30-year mortgage in the amount of $360,000 at 0 percent interest. Granted, these are extremes, but somewhere between them is a combination of price and terms that may work for many sellers. Finding the right combination is the art.

What do you think about rent-to-own deals?

We've never been involved in rent-to-own deals, so we're not the best people to answer this question. These types of deals are ones where all or part of the rent is applied toward a future purchase. This can be a way for buyers with little or no money to accumulate down payments gradually. Some people have done quite well with it. Mike had a real estate agent in his area that for years sold properties for 10 percent down and financed the purchases on a contract for deed. He kept taking the houses back and reselling them over and over. When he passed away recently, there were over 150 of these in his estate. Mike tried to buy them, but his heirs would only offer to sell them the same way. Mike passed on the deal because he didn't feel it was right for him.

Do houses with fireplaces rent better?

It all depends on the area. Naturally, fireplaces in Arizona and south Florida are not as desirable as they are in Minnesota and Maine. We find that while fireplaces make properties more desirable in some areas, they also come with problems. With wood-burning fireplaces, tenants aren't as careful about watching out for stray sparks that may pop out onto carpets or cleaning up ashes and debris that can be costly to a landlord. On the other hand, gas logs can be an asset without the mess associated with wood-burning fireplaces.

What about trailers or trailer parks? Would you recommend them for new investors?

We recommend investing in the parks but not in the trailers. Unlike houses, trailers go down in value. Renting the sites for mobile homes is fairly simple. The biggest difference between that and renting single-family houses is that you will need to factor in the cost of common-area maintenance (mowing, snow removal, etc.) and area lighting that probably will be your responsibility. In some parks, the landlord also furnishes water. If this is the case, you will need to factor that expense in as well.

What do you think about buying foreclosed mobile homes, selling them, and holding the notes?

Mobile homes are not like houses at all. They are more like automobiles. Unlike houses, they depreciate rather than appreciate. There may be money to be made by selling mobile homes and carrying the financing, but that's not part of the Weekend Millionaire method of wealth building. Mike once bought a mobile home park and got two of the mobile homes with the purchase. When the first one went vacant, he hauled it off and trashed it. Now he just rents the lot.

When the monthly payment way exceeds net operating income (NOI), is that an indication that you don't want the property as a rental?

The answer to this question is simple: Why would anyone want to own a property that is going to eat into their income? We call these properties "alligators." Many people have suffered serious financial losses because they bought alligators hoping that inflation would bail them out of the negative cash flow before their money ran out.

I remember listening to one of Carleton Sheets' audiotapes, and he said, "Stay away from two bedrooms." What do you think about two-bedroom homes as rentals?

Stick with Bread-and-Butter Properties

What Carleton was talking about is that three-bedroom homes are better, not that two-bedroom homes are not good rentals. Anyone who would rent a two-bedroom home could rent a three-bedroom home, and most people looking for a four-bedroom home probably could squeeze into a three-bedroom home if they needed to. This is what makes three-bedroom homes more versatile rentals.

In some blue-collar towns, home values rise slower. Also, if the towns aren't managed right, perhaps values won't rise much at all or even will drop. How does this factor into the overall buy-and-hold strategy to generate income?

If you buy right, even if the property never goes up in value, you still will make money, just not as much. The rate of appreciation is of concern primarily to speculators . . . people who buy expecting to sell for a profit. You make money when the rent goes up and the mortgage pays down. If the rates don't go up, the mortgages still pay down.

Wouldn't you agree that the big monthly rents come from commercial/ multiunit properties?

Big rents are certainly more likely from these properties, but we'd rather have $10,000-per-month income from ten $1,000-per-month rentals than from one $10,000-per-month unit. The risk is spread out better, and we believe that you should stay away from the larger properties until you gain more experience and build a solid base with bread-and-butter properties. Granted, cash flow goes up dramatically the more units there are at a given location, but so does the risk. The temptations to buy large multiunit properties is great, but keep in mind that if something happens that causes the property or the area to become undesirable suddenly, a large multiunit property might drag you and your entire portfolio down with it.

How do you feel about duplexes compared with single-family rentals?

Duplexes are great, but there are differences from single-family homes. Expenses such as common-area maintenance and utilities often come into play with any multifamily property, even if it is just a duplex. Just be sure to factor in these added expenses when computing net operating income (NOI) so that you don't end up paying too much.

What is the most expensive home you will buy for a rental?

Prices can vary widely from market to market. A house that will sell for $100,000 in one market may go for $250,000 in another market. As long as you avoid the lower 25 percent and upper 25 percent of the rent range and use rents in the middle 25 to 75 percent to determine values, you should be okay. Properties that can be purchased with a calculated net operating income (NOI) in the middle range of rents make the best rentals, and the closer you get to the exact middle, the better.

How do you figure out what is upscale and what is a slum that I should avoid?

The best way is to look at the properties, but conversations with good property managers in the area will help a great deal in making that determination. They know the areas that should be avoided, as well as the ones that are best for rentals.

9

Learn Your Market

In Chapter 9 of *The Weekend Millionaire's Secrets to Investing in Real Estate*, we discussed the importance of learning your market. We equated this to the early pioneers who sent out scouts to survey what lay ahead. Our suggestion that you focus on an area within a 10-mile radius of where you live brought a variety of questions, especially from people living in such major markets as New York and Los Angeles.

We must apologize for not explaining that the 10-mile radius does not work in all areas. In major metropolitan areas where demand for close-in living puts intense pressure on the market and pushes prices up unrealistically when compared with most areas of the country, you may have to go further out from the cities to find good deals.

Here are some of the questions we have received about this chapter.

I haven't purchased anything yet, but I'm working with an agent who deals in foreclosure. How can I find some of the good deals you talk about before they go into foreclosure?

One of the biggest reasons for getting out and riding around in the the area where you plan to invest is to meet people and learn what's going on in the neighborhoods. There are very few properties that make it to foreclosure without the neighbors knowing there is a problem months before the property is actually foreclosed on. Many times during your rides you will see properties that appear to be vacant, yards that haven't been mowed in weeks, and even "For Sale by Owner" signs that give indications that something is not right. When you find these situations, simply stopping and talking with a neighbor often can produce a wealth of information that can help you make a deal. It's easy to start a conversation with a simple question such as, "I'm interested in buying in the area, and I noticed that the house next door appears to be vacant, abandoned, unkempt, or for sale [or whatever other indicator you spot], and I was just wondering what you might know about it?" Another suggestion: If you're a member of a church or temple, let your priest, minister, or rabbi know that you're a real estate investor. Often they hear of members of their congregations who are in financial trouble.

Do you do any kind of marketing to get leads in the area where you want to invest?

Your best marketing tool is your business card. By simply getting to know the people within the area and giving them a card, you let them know that you are an investor who wants to invest in the area, and the card gives them a way to get in touch with you. It's always good to give people two or three cards and ask them to pass them on to people they know who may need to sell their property. By having an extra card or two, they can give one away and still keep one for themselves.

You mention stopping and talking with people in the neighborhoods you are farming as being a good way to learn about situations that may be good deals. I find it difficult to start a conversation with someone I don't know. Is there a good way to do this?

We're amazed at the amount of information you can pick up by starting a conversation simply by saying, "Hi, I'm _____, and I'm interested in this neighborhood. What can you tell me about it?" A good follow-up is, "Do you know any people who are planning to sell their home?" People typically love to talk about their community and their neighbors and often will divulge many good tips you can use. Let them know that you are an investor and not a real estate agent looking for listings.

What are some of the important things that I should try to find out about when I'm talking with people in the neighborhoods?

Find out what people like and dislike about the area, whether or not there are problem neighbors, if there is public water and sewer, if there are any traffic problems, if the streets are public or private, the ratio of renters to owners in the neighborhood, how quickly properties in the area sell, if there is anyone having difficulties that might cause them to need to sell quickly, and any additional information you can think of that will help you to determine if the neighborhood is a good place to invest.

There seems to be a lot of people who focus totally on "For Sale by Owner" (FSBO) properties. Do you find that you can get better deals with these properties than with ones listed with real estate agents?

There are a few good FSBO deals, just as there are a few good deals listed with real estate agents. We certainly wouldn't recommend that you focus totally on FSBOs because if you do, you will miss out on many good brokered deals. There are a number of reasons for FSBOs not being good deals. Owners could be asking a price that is higher than a broker would be willing to list the property for. Sometimes it's an FSBO because the seller doesn't have enough equity to pay a broker's commission. The biggest reason we find FSBOs difficult to deal with is the seller's emotional involvement. Until sellers become desperate, most hold out hopes of getting a high price and are insulted by wholesale offers.

I have been talking with a couple of property wholesalers. These are people who find properties, get them under contract, and then flip them to investors without ever actually taking ownership. They get properties on the courthouse steps or at bank foreclosure sales and then sell them to investors. Do you think that this is a good way to find properties?

There's nothing wrong with buying from wholesalers if you can get good deals, but if you're riding your markets regularly and keeping up with what is going on in the various neighborhoods, chances are you'll know about the deals before the wholesalers do.

Speaking of foreclosures, do you have any tips for finding them?

There are several ways to find foreclosures, but probably one of the most effective ways is to visit the county courthouse on a regular basis and check the filings. Once again, as with the answer to the preceding question, keeping up with what's happening in the area where you are investing is the best way to locate owners with problems before their properties go into foreclosure.

I understand the idea of buying property within a 10-mile radius of my home; however, in my city, property taxes are astronomical and only getting higher. My 1,700-square-foot house costs me $330 per month in property taxes. The same 1,700-square-foot house 60 miles west of here would cost only about $19 per month in property taxes. What would you do in this situation?

In situations such as yours, you may need to look further out to find deals that will generate cash flow, but rather than expanding to a much larger radius around where you live, the next-best suggestion is to create a 10-mile radius in the area where you want to invest. The purpose of the 10-mile radius is to provide an area to farm that is large enough to contain many properties but small enough so that your investments do not become so scattered that it is burdensome and time-consuming to check on them.

When I get out and ride the area I have chosen to farm, I see signs everywhere that say "I Buy Ugly Houses," "Quick Cash for Your Home," "Avoid Foreclosure," "I Buy for Cash—Quick Closings," and more. Should I be concerned that there are too many people getting into real estate investing?

You can bet that the people putting up those signs are not investors but speculators. They are the people who are trying to buy cheap and quickly flip the properties for a few dollars profit. We've been investing for many years and have seen new "investors" come and go by the hundreds. There always have been people wanting to get into real estate investing, but the vast majority of them do not take the time to learn how to do it right, and they fail to stick with it for the long haul the way a true investor would. Many of these wanna-be investors end up selling their properties wholesale just to get out.

What is the advantage to getting out and riding the same neighborhoods over and over rather than looking at new neighborhoods?

This is a bit like asking why a farmer goes back and cultivates his or her crop after he or she plants the seeds. Each week, each month, some properties sell, new ones go on the market, and people divorce, are transferred, have accidents, or retire, etc. Each neighborhood is constantly evolving and changing. By keeping abreast of what is taking place in the area you are farming, you enhance your opportunity to be first in line to take advantage of deals when they come along.

10

Don't Be Discouraged by Asking Prices

Everywhere we go we hear people talk about how much sellers are asking for this property or that property, and invariably, the discussion leads to a comment such as, "This is why we can't make the numbers work." Mike bought his first investment property in 1972, and every year since, as he kept buying more and more investment properties, people told him that prices were too high. Had he allowed this kind of talk to discourage him, there would be no *Weekend Millionaire* series of books.

When people talk with you about asking prices, just remember one thing, Weekend Millionaires look for a way, not an excuse. Asking prices are not selling prices, and even though some properties actually sell for more than the asking price, remember that unless you can find ways to buy properties that will have at least a breakeven cash flow, they are not investments but "alligators."

Here are some of the questions we have received from readers.

Prices are so high that finding deals that will generate cash flow seems to be nearly impossible. How do you find the wholesale deals?

Don't Be Discouraged by Asking Prices

Keep in mind that price is only part of the equation used to determine value; the other is terms. During boom periods, when demand is pushing up prices for conventional buyers, you need to focus more on negotiating wholesale terms. The time to focus on price is when the market is soft and people are desperate to sell. Whatever the market conditions, some people are more motivated by price, and some are more motivated by terms. The art of buying wholesale is finding out what motivates the seller.

Why would someone be willing to finance a sale of their property and negotiate wholesale terms when the market is booming and they could sell for cash?

Not everyone wants or needs cash. To an elderly person looking to convert real estate equity into income for retirement, cash on which they may have to pay tax and which they may only be able to invest at 2 to 3 percent interest may have little appeal. Taking back a mortgage that enables them to sell at a higher price and gives them a steady income may be more attractive than the cash.

Do you find that the percentage of sellers who finance is lower when bank interest rates are very low?

When interest rates on mortgages are low, the rates on deposits are also abysmally low. People who are relying on interest income for their retirement suffer. The incentive is greater for sellers to finance the purchases, and also, many people with money invested in CDs suddenly become great sources of mortgage money. They can pull money out of their banks, invest it in mortgages, and get much higher returns. In addition, the monthly payments on the mortgages become a good source of retirement income.

When the asking price is much higher than you can pay as an investor, don't you run the risk of being ridiculed if you make a low offer?

We'd like to answer this question with a question. Would you rather be laughed at for your wholesale offer, one you can support with the numbers, or go broke because you paid too much? No matter how low your offer may be, how much you are ridiculed for it, or how much it might offend the seller, the worst thing that can happen is that it is rejected. To be successful, investment properties must work for you, not place you in a situation where you have to work for them.

Is there any rule of thumb that I can use to give me some idea of how much sellers may come off their asking prices?

Keep in mind that since every property is different, every seller is different, and market conditions vary from one area to another, establishing a rule of thumb to determine how much sellers will come off their asking prices is impossible. What is important is to establish guidelines that will work for you, and then don't be tempted to violate them just because asking prices may seem high. We've actually made purchases that ranged from less than 50 percent of asking price to more than the asking price, yet all fit our established guidelines. How you structure your offers is far more important than the prices you offer.

What do you say to sellers who have a certified appraisal to support the price they are asking for their property?

An appraisal is an estimate of what a willing and informed seller will accept and a willing and informed buyer will pay when neither is under pressure, so it is only an estimate of the market value of a property on the day of the appraisal. You can't pay market value for properties and rent them for market value and expect to have a positive cash flow; you have to buy at wholesale. For this reason, you have to be patient, keep making offers, and find situations where there is not adequate time for the seller to find a willing buyer at market value. When you present a wholesale offer, be prepared to explain how you arrived at your price to counter the appraisal the seller is using to support his or her price.

PART III

How to Find the Ideal Seller

I t only stands to reason that this part of *The Weekend Millionaire's Secrets to Investing in Real Estate* would bring hundreds of questions. It was by no means meant to be an all-encompassing list of the many ways investors could find ideal sellers. It was designed to illustrate that there are as many different ways to buy as there are combinations of properties and people.

We have sorted through the questions and grouped them by the appropriate chapters in the real estate book, but in this part you may find questions that go beyond the topic of the chapter. We wanted to include questions that we felt were important to finding ideal sellers but didn't fit one of the actual chapter titles. As you learn more about investing the Weekend Millionaire way, you'll learn that ideal sellers come from all walks of life. For the rich or poor, the young or old, and everyone in between, situations create needs for people to sell properties quickly and under favorable circumstances for investors. The art is finding them before someone else does.

The situations that create flexible sellers are often embarrassing, humiliating, and generally uncomfortable for sellers to discuss. As an investor, be considerate of the fact that many sellers' financial dilemmas are not their fault. Accidents, injuries, illnesses, loss of employment, and other financially devastating events can occur through no fault of theirs. Things they can influence, such as business failures and divorce, often are the result of bad decision making, which is painful to acknowledge. Even people on the brink of bankruptcy often remain in a state of denial until the instigation of legal action forces them to face reality.

We understand their quandary and hope that throughout this part our answers reflect the importance of having empathy for sellers who may have run out of options. We are not there to take unfair advantage of them but to help them solve their problems, and the profit we make is our reward for doing so.

Finally, there are many other reasons that sellers become motivated—reasons that have nothing to do with financial desperation. One of the biggest opportunities we see in the coming years is helping retiring Baby Boomers convert real estate holdings into retirement incomes. Many of these people own properties free and clear and aren't in financial trouble, but they would like to supplement their retirement with income from the sale of their properties. The Weekend Millionaire way of investing will be increasingly attractive to Boomers as they begin to figure out that they can get higher prices when they sell by offering favorable terms with low interest rates. Low rates, especially 0 percent financing makes it impractical for an investor to refinance and pay off the loans early. Because investors won't want to pay off their loans early, seller are assured that they will have a continuing income stream from the sale of their properties.

So let's move on to answer questions about how to find the ideal seller.

11

The Seller Has Moved

When sellers move away from a property, for whatever reason, and find themselves trying to pay the expenses on a property they aren't using, they can become very motivated. Sellers who have moved are a great source of wholesale deals. In this chapter of our book *The Weekend Millionaire's Secrets to Investing in Real Estate*, Mike recounts the story of how he purchased a property from a young woman who married and moved out of state, leaving her with a property she tried to rent to a girlfriend.

As so often happens, the rental arrangement did not work out, and the girlfriend put the owner in a position that nearly caused her to lose the property in foreclosure. Unfortunately for the sellers, thousands of situations similar to this arise around the country each month. Sellers move, properties become vacant or abandoned, and opportunities abound for investors when they do.

Here are questions we have been asked about these types of properties.

How do you find properties where the owner has moved and is renting the property to help cover the mortgage?

How to Find the Ideal Seller

One way to do this is to watch the "For Rent" ads in the classified section of your local paper or other real estate publications and look for ads offering local properties with out-of-town phone numbers. This can be a good indication that the owner has relocated and has not been able to sell the house before moving. Another good way is to stop and talk with people within the communities where you want to invest. Ask them if they know of any houses where the owner has moved away and hasn't been able to sell.

When people are unable to sell a property before they move, is it usually because it needs a lot of repairs? Wouldn't that mean that you would have to put a lot of cash into the deal if you bought it?

Sometimes that's the case, but we find that it's the exception rather than the rule. The reasons we find that most people are unable to sell is because they are asking more for their property than it's worth. Most people have inflated opinions about the value of their property because they have emotional attachments that add value in their mind but don't add value for a buyer, especially an investor. This is the biggest reason that sellers become more flexible the longer the property is on the market. Eventually they come to realize that they have it overpriced.

What about abandoned properties? Do these make good prospective purchases for investors?

Abandoned properties, ones that the owners have walked away from for one reason or another, can become good rentals if you can get good title to them. An example of this is property that was owned by someone who died without a will, and the heirs can't agree on what to do with it. None of them want to fool with it, and no one wants to pay the taxes on it. Properties like this often are seized and sold for back taxes, but even if you buy them at the tax sale, most of the time the owners will have a lengthy redemption period before you can be assured of good title.

If you locate a property that is in an estate with multiple heirs, how do you go about making an offer for it? To whom do you make the offer?

These properties can be difficult but certainly not impossible to purchase. Often you can go to the local court house and find out who is receiving the property tax bills and start with that person. Eventually, someone is going to end up with the property. Why not you? This brings to mind the difference between successful people and unsuccessful people. Successful people do the things unsuccessful people either can't or won't do. Purchasing properties that have difficulties is not easy, but it can be very rewarding. Learn to look for a way, not an excuse. By all means read our book *Weekend Millionaire Mindset: How Ordinary People Can Achieve Extraordinary Success*.

Are there abandoned properties where the mortgage or note holders just don't choose to pick up the property to protect their position? Is that a frequent occurrence?

Not necessarily. Even if they leave the property, the owners might still pay the mortgage because they want to keep their credit clean. They may not be able to afford to live in the property and would like to sell it to stop the bleeding of money going out. They may not be able to live in it because they don't have the money to fix it up and make it habitable. This is where you might be able to find some good deals.

How do you find abandoned properties?

One of the easiest ways to find abandoned properties is to do what we advocate that you do on a regular basis . . . get out and ride the areas where you want to invest. You can easily spot houses that are vacant and unkempt. Another good way is to let everyone know that you're looking for vacant, run-down properties.

I can understand how death can cause a property to become abandoned, but what are some of the reasons living people would move off and abandon their property?

There are many reasons among which are divorce, job loss, job transfer, illness, accidents, age, and any other reason that might place an owner in a position where he or she can't maintain the property. Some heirs actually inherit properties so far away that they don't want them and don't want to complicate their lives by trying to maintain them until they can be sold.

What about sellers who move and don't abandon their property? Are these good prospects for investors to pursue?

Absolutely, because the vast majority of people who move and leave a house vacant do so because they haven't been able to sell it. The longer it sits on the market, the more flexible these sellers become. There are few forces stronger than having to make payments on vacant property that will motivate sellers to reduce the price, accept owner financing, offer favorable terms, or whatever else they need to do to move the property. Often they will try to rent the property to help cover the payment only to discover that long-distance property management can be a real hassle.

What's the best way to deal with sellers who have moved?

First, keep it very simple! Realize that these properties can be real headaches for the owners. Many times they will owner finance, which means no points and no fees, and they frequently don't care whether you have a job, money, or credit. They eventually reach a point where they just want the headache to stop. Make offers that will work for you regardless of what they are asking. We've made many offers that were summarily rejected in the beginning only to have the seller come back months later to see if the offer is still good. Buying properties from sellers who have moved is no different from buying properties from people who have become motivated sellers for any other reason.

12

Sellers Have Divorced

Divorce is seldom a pleasant experience for anyone, especially the two people involved; unfortunately, it happens all too frequently and often leaves bitterness and emotional scars that are slow to heal. Since real estate is usually owned jointly with a spouse, properties often are used as pawns as one aggrieved party tries to hurt the other. Anger vented through the illogical disposition of real property can produce excellent opportunities for investors.

We don't advocate that you try to take advantage of people, but in a divorce situation, the parties often are willing to sacrifice equity just to get out of the marriage and dissolve the relationship. When situations such as this arise, someone is going to get a good deal. Why shouldn't it be you? This may look to you like ambulance-chasing lawyers who visit the hospital rooms of accident victims. Understand that buying from people who are divorcing does not mean that you have to take advantage of them.

The story we told in this chapter is a perfect example of how bitterness and animosity can linger between divorced couples for years when property is not liquidated quickly. By taking the time to discover the feelings of both parties and to learn about the differing needs they each had, Mike was able to secure a wholesale purchase while meeting the needs of both sellers.

Here are questions our readers have asked about buying properties from divorcing couples.

Why wouldn't couples getting a divorce list their property with a real estate broker and try to get as much for it as possible?

All too often the incidents that lead up to the divorce produce so much anger and hostility that the parties are unwilling to work together to get a good price. In most cases there is a mortgage on the property, and someone has to make the payments while the property is being marketed. In situations such as this, the party who feels scorned is seldom willing to contribute anything toward making the loan payments. This is one of the reasons that divorcing couples find themselves in a position of having to sell quickly at a deep discount to avoid foreclosure.

Is it okay to approach couples you know are having problems even before they file for divorce?

We wouldn't recommend that you approach couples having problems with some crude question such as, "I hear you're getting a divorce, do you want to sell your house cheap?" However, there's certainly nothing wrong with letting them know about your interest with a simple, "I'm interested in buying in your neighborhood. Could I give you one of my cards, and if you know of any houses that may be coming on the market, would you call me? I'm an investor, and I can usually close very quickly if I can get a good deal." There's no need to mention that you know they are having problems. If their situation deteriorates to the point that they file for divorce, they will have your contact information, and chances are good that they will give you a call.

When making an offer to buy property from a divorced couple, which one do you approach to present your offer?

In situations such as this, it's often best to use a third party such as a buyer's agent to present your offer. While there are situations like the one we describe in our real estate book, unless you are an experienced negotiator and investor, it's very easy for one of the parties to get the impression that you favor the other and balk at your offer. The third party can act as an independent mediator to prevent the sellers from pulling you into the middle of their dispute.

Are there risks involved when you buy from divorcing couples before their divorce is finalized?

Not if both parties sign the deed at closing, and you are able to obtain title insurance. You should never buy property from anyone without having a real estate attorney or title company do a thorough title search and obtain insurance against title defects.

What about buying from one member of a divorcing couple if that person holds the property in his or her name only?

This is a legal question best answered by an attorney licensed to do business in the state where the property is located. There are some situations where one spouse has the right to sell without the permission or concurrence of the other, but these usually result from having a properly drafted and legally recorded prenuptial agreement granting this right or when the properties are held in other legal entities such as partnerships, limited liability corporations (LLCs), etc., and the selling spouse has been granted the right to act on behalf of the entity. In cases such as this, always consult an attorney before closing the deal, and be sure to obtain title insurance.

How do I avoid the feeling that I'm taking advantage of other people's misfortune when trying to buy from a divorced couple or one that is going through a divorce?

You are not the reason the couple is having problems. One or both of them may try to pull you into their dispute looking for sympathy, but you must remain objective and look at the transaction as strictly a business deal. The fact that they are having problems and stand to lose a substantial portion of their equity in the process is not your problem. If you let yourself feel sorry for them and allow this feeling to influence your decisions, you are taking on their problems. The circumstances that forced them to sell at a reduced price will not be changed by your sympathy. If the need exists for them to dispose of a property quickly and you are able to facilitate this disposition, you may be doing them a great favor by taking the property off their hands so that they can get on with their separate lives. You should never allow other people's problems to cause you to feel bad.

What if I get a contract to purchase a property from a divorcing couple and one of them changes his or her mind before the closing? Can they go to court to stop the sale?

Usually, a purchase agreement signed by all parties and having monetary consideration is a binding contract, and if one party tries to renege, that party can be compelled to go through with the deal or face monetary damages. This is another one of those circumstances that can happen when dealing with divorce situations and is a question best answered by a competent attorney. Just realize that divorce is a stressful event for people and that they often make irrational decisions as a result of the stress.

13

Seller Has High Equity in the Property

Sellers with high equities or ones who own their properties free and clear have many more options than those who have little or no equity. Before the advent of the due-on-sale clause in mortgages, investors looked for sellers with assumable loans and little or no equity and often would get seller financing for their equity as a way to make no-money-down purchases. Today it's just the opposite; the more equity a seller has, the better the chance for an investor to make a no-money-down purchase.

While no money down sounds great, it's not necessarily the best option for a buy-and-hold investor. There are many properties that can be purchased for no money down that you can't afford to own after you buy them. We like to find sellers with high equity for a different reason: They have the ability to offer favorable terms that can allow you to structure wholesale deals even when you have to get part of the financing from a conventional lender.

The answer to the following questions will help you to understand this concept better.

How to Find the Ideal Seller

Why does finding sellers with high equity help you to structure better deals?

We think that you overlook some great opportunities when you assume that it will take more cash to deal with sellers who have high equity. These sellers actually have many more options when they sell. One of the best techniques we know for new investors to get started is to find a property with high equity; obtain a small first mortgage to pay off existing financing, pay the real estate agent's commission, and even give the seller some cash; and then ask the seller to carry back a large second mortgage for the balance. There are many such opportunities just waiting for someone to grab them.

Do you find that the percentage of sellers who finance is lower during a strong seller's market?

No, if anything, we find that the percentage is higher during a sellers' market. The very low interest rates that have produced the strong sellers' market also have caused people with money to seek ways to earn more on their money than the banks are paying. As a result, many sellers who are looking to downsize or to dispose of investment properties are willing to carry financing rather than putting cash into money-market accounts or certificates of deposit (CDs).

What about the risks that go along with owner financing? Won't sellers be concerned about selling to someone who may default on the mortgage?

Granted, there aren't too many risks for buyers but a lot for sellers, so you have to do a good job of selling yourself as an honest and reliable person. You have to do the same thing when you borrow from banks, but usually it's easier to do with sellers because they have a vested interest in being flexible because they want to sell the property. If you are in a position to put some cash into the deal, it will make the seller more willing to finance.

By now I'm sure you guys have so many leads flowing in to you that you don't have to market anymore. But for those of us without the connections yet, what are the top three ways you are finding sellers with lots of equity?

Sure, the top three ways are (1) Make offers! (2) Make offers! (3) Make offers! Ask for seller financing in your offers, and see what happens. All sellers will tell you that they want cash if you ask, but until you present them with an offer, you don't know for sure what they will do. It's harder to get information about a seller's equity than it used to be when this information was listed in the Multiple Listing Service (MLS), but making offers that ask for financing is probably the best way to find out what a seller can do.

Can you also ask for seller financing on properties listed in a Multiple Listing Service (MLS), or does it apply only to "For Sale by Owner" properties?

You can ask for seller financing from anyone . . . even banks that are trying to sell REO (real estate owned by banks) properties. Don't be afraid to ask. The worst thing a seller can do is say "No."

When you ask for seller financing from banks (REOs), do they need proof of funds?

When banks sell REO (real estate owned by banks) properties and provide financing, they are going to treat you the same as if you were applying for a new loan. If you have reservations about your credit score, forget the banks for a few months, and look for deals that you can make with seller financing. Sellers usually don't check your score. Problems obtaining conventional financing have killed the enthusiasm of more new investors than probably any other thing. There are dozens of ways to buy without conventional financing.

Do you recommend using alternative lenders offering niche products that serve investors? Are they a good source of funds for new investors?

We're not sure what you mean by alternative lenders offering niche products for investors, but there are many private investors looking for a place to shift money out of bank CDs into higher-yielding, secure investments. Real estate mortgages are one of the most secure investments available for them. If you're talking about some of the hard-money lenders who charge very high rates, we feel that these are more appropriate for people buying fixer-uppers or flipping properties. A buy-and-hold investor would not find these lenders attractive owing to the high interest rates they typically charge.

How to Find the Ideal Seller

What's your opinion on no-money-down deals? Are they worth looking for in today's market?

No money down was a great concept when underlying loans were assumable. It's much harder to do these days. And of course it's very hard to make the numbers work the way we teach. When Robert Allen wrote *No Money Down,* buyers tried to find sellers with very little equity in order to make a deal. Today, no-money-down deals are much easier made with sellers who have large equities or own the property free and clear. By all means, if you can find no-money-down deals that work according to our teachings, buy them. These will be the most profitable deals you can make because of the high leverage. The biggest problem we find with no-money-down deals today is that many of them have problems that make them difficult to continue owning after you purchase them. Just be careful. If a deal looks too good to be true . . . it probably is.

I've been told to find a portfolio lender because they are more flexible. What are portfolio lenders, and why are they more flexible?

"Portfolio loans" are loans that banks plan to keep in their investment portfolio. Most mortgage loans are sold in the secondary market, and they must meet rigid guidelines to qualify. When a bank makes a portfolio loan, it does have more flexibility in the underwriting process because it doesn't have to meet those guidelines. Usually these loans are given only to their very best customers, the ones the banks don't have to worry about. If you're just getting started and need a nonconforming loan, a bank that would make you a portfolio loan probably will charge a much higher interest rate to do so.

I have a neighbor who is selling her house for about $150,000, and her current mortgage is about $800 a month (with insurance and property taxes included). If I assume her loan, can I get the bank to quit impounding the insurance and property taxes so that my payments would be less?

You must be talking about making an offer "subject to" an existing mortgage and having the owner continue to make payments on it. You cannot assume mortgages any more without qualifying unless the mortgage is a very old one that was taken out before the addition of the due-on-sale clause contained in today's mortgages. If you try to assume the loan without telling the lender, the lender can call the full amount of the loan due as soon as it finds out. Some states are now considering legislation that would make it a violation of law not to fully disclose such a transaction to the lender. Stay away from transactions that call for you to assume an existing loan without telling the lender. You will be able to get your payments down by getting a new loan with a longer term.

I'm really confused about owner financing. If I buy a house for $100,000 and make my mortgage payments to the bank and after living there five years I pay it down to $95,000 but I would like to sell it and move, how would I owner finance the deal if I hadn't paid my debt to the bank?

An owner can only finance the amount of his or her equity. Offers asking for owner financing only work if the seller has significant equity in the property. In the example you cite, where you would be the seller, it sounds like you are talking about wrap-around financing, which we don't recommend. (See the preceding answer.) To provide owner financing, a buyer would need to obtain a new loan, and then you may be able to offer owner financing for that portion of the sale between the buyer's loan and the amount at which you sell the property, provided that you have that much equity in the property.

I can understand retirees with no mortgage being flexible if they want to move and are looking for an income stream, but with other scenarios it seems like sellers are taking unnecessary risk with little reward if they owner finance. How can you make a seller comfortable that you will be able to make the payments?

There are many situations other than retirement that make sellers willing to carry financing. Inherited property, job loss, illness or accident, and other events can create situations where sellers are willing to take back financing in order to rid themselves of what they perceive to be problem properties. Many times they are willing to take risks to accomplish this. Occasionally, you will find sellers willing to accept a little risk to convert equity into an income stream, especially if the income stream is better than what they can get from other investments.

How to Find the Ideal Seller

I recently purchased Carleton Sheets' Real Estate Toolkit and was playing around with the calculator it contains, trying to figure out how balloon payments work. I thought if I tried different numbers that by looking at the results I could figure it out. When I hit the amortization button, it doesn't show me past the "balloon period."

The reason it doesn't show you anything past the "balloon period" is because there is nothing past it. When the balloon period is over, you will owe the full remaining principal due at that time unless you can renegotiate the loan. Usually, a lender will renew the loan for an additional period if you have performed satisfactorily during the original term, but the lender doesn't have to. We actually have had a bank refuse to renew loans that were paid impeccably during the original period because the bank found itself over-loaded with real estate loans and was ordered by regulators to purge a significant number of them to balance its portfolio.

14

Converting Home Equity into Retirement Income

The importance of converting home equity into retirement income is going to become stronger and stronger as the Baby Boom generation enters retirement. A growing number of these people will find themselves short of funds to live the lifestyle to which they have become accustomed and will start looking for ways to supplement Social Security payments or other retirement incomes. The equity they have accumulated in real estate is going to provide them with one of their few sources of additional income.

Many Boomers have lived a "keep-up-with-the-Jones" lifestyle, and the only wealth they have accumulated is the equity in their homes . . . homes that often tend to be larger than they need in retirement. Converting this equity into retirement income is going to provide wonderful opportunities for investors seeking long-term investments in real estate.

Buying from people who want to convert equity into retirement income results in real win-win opportunities in which the goals of both sellers and buyers can be met without either feeling that they have had to sacrifice to put the deals together. The questions we have received concerning this emerging opportunity are varied and bring up some interesting points.

If a seller carries back a loan, is there a third party involved, such as an escrow company? Also, who keeps "official" track of payments and balance due and year-end tax info, etc.?

If you are in a "deed of trust" state, there is a third party, namely, the holder of the trust deed. This can be the closing attorney, a title company, or anyone the seller designates. It even could be a son, daughter, or friend of the seller. The note is the evidence of the debt, and the recorded trust deed or mortgage is the security for the debt. It is held by the trustee until the debt has been paid, and he or she can record a release of the encumbrance. When a seller finances the purchase, it is best for the closing attorney or title company to provide both parties with an amortization schedule for the loan. This schedule shows the amount of principal and interest that make up each payment and the balance due after each payment is made. The buyer should mark the date and check number beside each payment as it is made, and the seller should mark the date and check number beside each payment as it is received. In this way both parties can keep up with everything needed for tax preparation without having to rely on the other. We also suggest that you reconcile your records with each other annually. Property taxes are a separate matter that does not involve the trustee.

Sounds good, so the Internal Revenue Service (IRS) will believe your numbers for taxes at year end as well, without any official docs?

You don't need a statement from a bank to satisfy the IRS. All you need are the documents to support the information on your tax return, and if questioned, you can provide canceled checks and the amortization schedule. We circle each principal and interest payment as we make it and post the check number we paid it with beside that line. One interesting thing about seller financing, you can make virtually any kind of payment arrangement you both agree on. It is not like bank financing that has to meet certain guidelines.

Can you assume a home-equity loan that is on a property you are purchasing, and if so, are there any risks associated with doing this?

Converting Home Equity into Retirement Income

We've never heard of home-equity loans being assumable. In every instance we've been involved with, the home-equity loan was paid off at closing.

I am looking at two different properties. One of them has a home-equity loan, and the other has a home-equity line of credit. What is the difference between a loan and a line of credit?

Both home-equity loans and home-equity lines of credit are usually second-mortgage loans. (They could also be first-mortgage loans or even third-mortgage loans. It depends on the number of loans on the property. They get their ranking from the date they were recorded.) The home-equity loan is usually an amortizing loan, whereas a line of credit is typically an interest-only loan that can be paid down and drawn back up as often as the borrower wants. Lines of credit usually have to be renewed more frequently than the amortizing loans.

What is a "direct principal reduction" loan?

A direct principle reduction loan is a 0 percent interest loan. The payor is paying off the principal without the payee adding any interest. There is no advantage to paying off a loan of this type early because the full remaining total of the payments is due at payoff.

If you use a direct principal reduction loan in order to meet a seller's asking price, don't you put yourself in a position where it is difficult, if not impossible, to sell the property until the loan is nearing payoff?

Fully amortizing direct principal reduction loans are wonderful tools for the long-term investor, but even if you don't plan to sell, we recommend that you insist on the note containing a substitution of collateral clause, an assumption clause, or both. These clauses give you the right to substitute another property of equal or greater value and keep the loan in the event of a sale or to allow the purchaser to assume the loan. In either case, direct principal reduction loans can be an aid to selling rather than a hindrance.

I want to start making offers using direct principle reduction loans. Who are the most likely sellers to give me these loans?

How to Find the Ideal Seller

We find that these loans are more attractive to older people wanting to trade real estate equity for an income stream to supplement their retirement. With a 0 percent loan they can sell their house for more money without having to worry about interest rates dropping a couple of points and having the loan paid off early. Only a fool would pay off a 0 percent interest loan early.

If a seller accepts a direct principal reduction loan as part of the sale of his or her property, won't the Internal Revenue Service (IRS) impute interest on the payments, and won't this interest be taxed at a higher rate than the capital-gains rate?

Yes, there would be imputed interest on the payments, but unless the seller has significant taxable income, the tax rate on the imputed interest and the tax rate on capital gains are virtually the same. Even in cases where there is some tax liability, it is usually not significant. We advise sellers to consult with a competent tax advisor if they have concerns.

What can you tell me about reverse mortgages? How do they work, and why are they attractive to some people?

They are called "reverse mortgages" because they work in reverse to conventional mortgages. To overly simplify this, instead of making payments to the mortgage holder, which reduces the balance owed on the loan, the mortgage holder makes payments to you, and the outstanding balance grows each month. The advantage is that you get an income or relief from making payments and get to keep living in the home. The disadvantage is that in the end, your heirs will have to pay off the mortgage if they want to keep the property. There are a number of plans ranging from equal monthly payments for a fixed period or for as long as the house remains your permanent residence, a line of credit to draw on when you need it, or modified plans consisting of combinations of these options.

My parents are 62 and 71 years of age. Their house payment is $1,300 per month (including taxes and insurance) with a 7 percent loan. They can't afford this anymore and are considering a reverse mortgage. Do you have any suggestions?

Converting Home Equity into Retirement Income

Their age is okay because you have to be 62 to qualify for a reverse mortgage, but we suggest that they meet with a counselor who can fully advise them of the ramifications. You may want to accompany them to the meeting because a reverse mortgage will affect your inheritance, assuming they plan to leave part or all of their estate to you when they pass away. Reverse mortgages are not for everyone, and seeking competent counsel is very important before entering into such an agreement.

You talk a lot about direct principal reduction or 0 percent loans. What if a seller wants interest on the loan?

If the seller wants interest, no problem; you simply have to adjust the amount of the loan downward to accommodate the percentage interest the seller wants. When the seller sees how much less he or she can get by insisting on interest, he or she often reconsiders. What we find is that when a seller counters a direct principal reduction loan request by offering to finance but requests interest, you have accomplished two things. First, you have learned that he or she can finance the purchase. Second, the seller has opened a negotiation in which you can adjust loan amounts, interest rates, and length of loan to give the seller the price he or she wants and still stay within the net operating income (NOI) the property will produce.

How common is it to find sellers willing to finance?

Believe it or not, nearly half of all real estate in this country is owned free and clear. Finding sellers able to finance all or a significant part of a purchase is not at all uncommon; finding sellers willing to do so is another matter. The better job you are able to do of convincing sellers that you are trustworthy and reliable, the better your chances of getting them to finance your purchases. This is one of the reasons we stress the importance of building a track record of performance. In the beginning, getting financing from banks or sellers is going to be difficult. Once you obtain financing, be sure to pay in a timely way and take proper care of the properties if you want to establish the kind of track record that builds confidence with both banks and sellers. Once you have proven that you can perform adequately through a full economic cycle or two, things will get significantly easier.

15

Sellers in Financial Trouble

As unfortunate as it may be, many people encounter unforeseen problems and/or make poor decisions that cause them to get in financial trouble. When this happens, they often find themselves desperate to unload real estate in an effort to remove the burden of mortgage payments, taxes, insurance, maintenance, upkeep, and other expenses. When faced with a choice among foreclosure, bankruptcy, and a discounted sale, most people will choose the discounted sale, which presents great opportunities for investors.

Don't view this as taking advantage of other people's misfortune. When people find themselves in financial difficulty, they eventually become resigned to the fact that they are going to lose their property one way or another. Then the question becomes, "How?" Will they lose it in foreclosure or bankruptcy, which will destroy their credit, or will they agree to a discounted sale that costs them most or all of their equity but may salvage their credit?

Situations such as this are never easy for the sellers, but they may have no other alternatives. You always should proceed with these transactions with this understanding: Try to leave the sellers with as much dignity as possible. Although they may be in a position where you can squeeze the last dollar from the transaction, you will be much better served by giving them a fair price, one you can live with but one that doesn't leave them feeling that you stole their property. If you can leave them feeling that you helped them rather than took advantage of their unfortunate situation, they will be much more likely to recommend you to others.

Here are answers to your questions about buying from people in financial trouble.

Have you ever offered to take over payments for a seller in distress?

We assume that you are talking about assuming a seller's loan as part of the purchase. What we usually do in cases such as this is to ask the sellers to give their lenders permission to talk with us about their loans. Then we can get first-hand information about the status of the loans and discuss the terms under which the bank would let us assume them. We have purchased properties in which we were allowed to catch up the sellers back payments and then assume their loans with no additional expense. Lenders become very flexible on their assumption policies when faced with deciding between foreclosing on a property or letting a creditworthy buyer assume the loan.

Any suggestions on how to go about purchasing a property when the sellers want to sell it and then rent it back from you?

The story in Chapter 15 of *The Weekend Millionaire's Secrets to Investing in Real Estate* discusses a successful transaction where we allowed the seller to stay in the property. We've done it a couple of times, and both have turned out very well. Both times it allowed the owners to cash out equity to clear up debts without having to move. Consider whether or not the sale of the property is going to improve the seller's finances substantially. If the sellers are able to get substantial equity out of the property and use it to clear up the problems that got them into financial trouble, renting back to them is much more attractive. If the sale of the property is only going to get them out of making a mortgage payment, you cannot expect them to be a good renter when they will have to make a rent payment to you that will be greater than the mortgage payment they were unable to make to the lender.

How to Find the Ideal Seller

Are there any dangers I should be on the lookout for when buying from a seller in financial trouble? I've heard some horror stories about people who trashed their property when they knew they were going to lose it anyway.

We've heard some of the same kinds of horror stories, but they seem to be more related to people losing their homes in foreclosure or bankruptcy actions. If you have built rapport with the sellers and they feel that you are trying to help them out of a jam, they have every incentive to deliver the property in good condition. We recommend that you go by the property with your real estate agent or the sellers on the way to the closing and conduct a final inspection. Pay particular attention to such things as appliances that are to go with the property. It's very easy to remove stoves, refrigerators, microwaves, dishwashers, etc. and sell them later.

When a seller tells you he or she needs cash now, is there any way to get him or her to entertain an offer that includes a one-year or longer lease option closing in 90 days? The 90-day clause is to give me time to get it rented.

Each situation is different. This is why we suggest that you sit down with sellers and learn as much as possible about their circumstances. If they are struggling to make payments because they have moved and haven't sold the property, a lease option that removes the burden of the second payment may be attractive to them. If they are living in the property and struggling to keep up with the payments and have other creditors hounding them for money, getting them to enter into a lease-option arrangement is unlikely. It never hurts to make an offer and see what happens.

In your book you say making an all-cash offer sometimes will get you a great price on a property. How do you make a low-price offer to prospective sellers without upsetting them?

When we can't find out about a seller's motivation and don't know if the seller will entertain a low-price cash offer, we usually make two offers at the same time, one with the low cash price and another at a higher price that asks the seller to carry back very low or 0 percent financing. The way the seller reacts to these offers gives us a better idea of his or her circumstances and motivation.

Does that mean that the cash price is really low and that the higher offer is about at the top of the range you can offer based on the property's net operating income (NOI)?

That's true. The wider range in price you can make the two offers, the greater is the possibility of getting a response from the seller. A wide range in price indicates that you have a lot of flexibility in what you will pay if the seller has flexibility in how you have to pay it. The biggest problem with this type of offer for people in financial distress is that they may not have any flexibility to deal. This method works best when you don't know the seller's financial condition.

I looked at a two-bedroom, one-bath, single-family residence where the owner paid $59,000 one year ago. According to my net operating income (NOI) calculations, that's about what I can pay for it, but the seller needs to sell it for more to cover the real estate commission. Am I wasting my time offering the same amount the seller paid, or should I just move on to something else? (I can't pay more and stay within the NOI.)

Let's start with the basic definition of "value." It's what a willing buyer will pay a willing seller when both are informed and neither one is under pressure. It doesn't say anything about what the owner paid for the property. Depending on the seller's situation, he or she may be willing to take a loss to get rid of the property. Make the offer and see what happens.

What if neither of us is under pressure; I can't see the sellers taking less than they paid when they could just hold out until someone gives them what they want?

It's not always that simple. The cost to hold onto the property while waiting for a better offer can eat up any gain that might be realized. We suggest that you ignore what they paid and make a lower offer than you could and then move up during the negotiation. Make them work for any concessions you give. Offer what will work for you, and forget about what they paid.

How flexible are banks about working with customers prior to foreclosing on them? Will they make any concession to avoid having to go into foreclosure?

How to Find the Ideal Seller

Banks do not want to foreclose on real estate loans. If you can get involved prior to the foreclosure sale, they are often very flexible. Mike actually has had banks let him assume sellers' loans, cut the interest rate, and pay all the closing costs in order to get him on the loan in place of sellers who were about to go into foreclosure or bankruptcy. Just be sure that the seller vacates the property before closing so that you can get possession immediately. You don't want to buy a property and then be held up for months trying to evict the former owners.

I recently made an offer on a property that was listed for $60,000. I offered $47,500, but the sellers got another offer for $65,000, which they accepted. Today I got a call saying the financing had fallen through on the other offer, and they wanted to know if my offer was still good. Does this happen very often?

We've seen situations like this a few times, and in each case we lowered our offer a little and resubmitted it. Sometimes we were able to buy at the lower price, but on occasion we have been negotiated back up to our original offer. What's amazing in cases like this is that our original offer has suddenly moved from being unacceptable to now being the asking price. This is a nice position to be in when it happens.

I have a situation where the seller has lost her job and hasn't been able to find another one. She has exhausted her savings, and now her only asset is her home, which she owns free and clear. She has offered to sell it to me at a substantial discount, but I was wondering if I should offer her some cash and ask her to carry the balance in a mortgage? Wouldn't that help her more?

Here's a case where the seller is having financial difficulty but still has some options. She needs cash but probably could finance part of the purchase if she wanted. This is where a financial calculator such as the one we recommend in Carleton Sheets' Real Estate Toolkit comes in very handy. (The toolkit is available on our Web site weekendmillionaire.com.) You didn't give us any numbers, so we'll use a hypothetical appraised value of $100,000 for the property to answer your question. Let's assume that she has offered to sell you the property for $75,000 cash, which you will have to borrow from a bank at 7 percent interest for 15 years. Now let's look at another option. Suppose that you offered her $100,600 for the property and proposed to pay $25,000 cash at closing, which again you borrow from a bank at 7 percent interest for 15 years, and the balance of $75,600 payable at $420 per month for 15 years at 0 percent interest. Which would be the better deal for you? Under the first scenario, your payment on the $75,000 would be $674.12 per month for 180 months. Under the second scenario, your payment on the $25,000 would be $224.71 per month for 180 months, which when combined with the $420.00 monthly payment is only $644.71 per month, or $29.41 per month less than you would pay buying at $75,000. This second scenario may be more attractive to the seller because it gives her immediate cash plus an income for the next 15 years. You could even be negotiated up to a $105,000 purchase price and still pay less per month than you would at the $75,000 cash price.

16

Real Estate Owned by Banks

When banks acquire real estate through foreclosure actions or by deeds in lieu of foreclosure, these properties are considered liabilities rather than assets. The reason for this is that the money tied up in these properties is not earning any return. To help you better understand how this works, assume that you had money invested in a certificate of deposit (CD) that was paying you a monthly income that you needed to live. If you took the money out of that CD and bought a piece of real estate that didn't pay any return, as well as costing you additional money to pay taxes and other expenses, you would want to get rid of it as quickly as possible.

The same thing hold true for banks. When you deposit money with banks, they take that money and invest it in loans that pay a higher percentage interest than they are paying you for the use of your money. If the bank invests your money in a mortgage loan that goes into default and then ends up having to seize the property securing the loan in a foreclosure action, the bank finds itself in the same position we described in the preceding example, except that the bank would have the added expense of having to continue paying you for the use of your money.

This may be an oversimplification, but it should help you to understand why banks don't like to hold real estate any longer than necessary. The sooner they can convert real estate back into cash, the quicker they can make another loan and start receiving income. For this reason, they are often willing to be very flexible and in many cases even take losses to get rid of these properties.

Much has been said and written about buying foreclosures, but here are some of the questions our readers have asked about the subject.

Can you negotiate a sale with a bank while the owner is in default and before the bank actually forecloses on the property?

No; banks can't sell properties until they actually get title to them. They can do this through a foreclosure action or by receiving a deed in lieu of foreclosure. This doesn't mean that you can't ask the owners to give their bank permission to discuss their loan with you and then you asking to assume the loan under different terms than the original borrower had.

What is the average percentage below appraised value that a bank will accept when selling foreclosed properties?

We are not aware of any percentage below appraised value that banks will accept. Once they own a property, they are like any other seller in that they want to get all they can for it. Market conditions and the amount of real estate owned by a bank have more to do with what the bank will accept than any other factor. During a strong sellers' market, the bank may get full market price, whereas in soft market conditions, the bank may accept 50 percent of the appraised value or less.

Once a bank has foreclosed on a property, can it just sell the property, or does it have to auction it off?

If the bank is willing to settle for whatever it gets for the property, it can sell it any way it wants. However, if the bank plans to go after the former owner for a deficiency judgment (which is rare), it needs to be more cautious in the way it handles the sale. In these cases, the bank usually sells the property at auction.

How can you find out about real estate owned by banks? Do they publish a list, or is there some other way to find out about these properties?

Probably the largest listing of foreclosed properties is found at www.hud. gov/offices/hsg/sfh/reo/homes.cfm. On this site you can search all of the U.S. Department of Housing and Urban Development (HUD) homes for sale state by state right down to the ZIP codes. Many banks publish lists of REO (real estate owned by banks) properties, but probably the best way is to build solid relationships with banks and let them know what types of properties you are interested in buying. Also, there are specific real estate agents that handle HUD home sales; find out who handles these in your market, and contact them.

Is there a way to find out how much a bank has in a property before making the bank an offer?

In most cases you can visit the county courthouse and look up the amount of the original deed of trust or mortgage and when it was recorded. This doesn't tell you how much has been paid down, if any, but it can give you some idea. Sometimes a bank officer will tell you the amount of the loan on which the bank foreclosed, but we don't put a lot of faith in what they say. We still think that the best thing to do is calculate what the property is worth to you based on the net operating income (NOI) it will produce and then make your offer based on that.

An officer at my bank contacted me and said that he had been given authority by the owner of a property the bank was foreclosing on to negotiate a sale price with an investor, but the owner would have to give final approval on the price. He even said that if we are close, the bank would postpone the foreclosure sale for up to 30 days for a $150 fee. Does this sound right?

We've never heard of a bank officer doing this, but it could be a case where he is trying to help the seller avoid foreclosure and save the bank problems as well. If he has the authority to negotiate for the seller, then make them an offer that will work for you, and see what they say. Just remember that all offers should work for you—not the banks, not the sellers, not the brokers, but you. You're the one who will have to pay for it. If you are able to make a deal, be sure to have a thorough title search done before closing, and obtain title insurance.

What percentage of the purchase price will a bank finance when selling an REO property?

It all depends on who is buying! If you know your banker well and have a good relationship, you can get better terms that someone walking in off the street trying to make his or her first transaction. There are no set guidelines banks have to follow, so technically, they can do what they want, but the closer they can get to making a loan that will qualify for sale in the secondary market, the easier it will be to get them to finance the purchase.

I tried to buy an REO property from my bank, but it told me that I would need to get my financing elsewhere? Why?

It could be because any favorable terms the bank gives will cause the loan to be classified as a "loan to facilitate" and have to be handled differently on the bank's books. The bank will have to set aside a higher percentage loan-loss reserve because of the favorable terms it has given, and the loans are not as easy for the bank to sell on the secondary market.

Wouldn't I find the best deals by watching the foreclosure notices and then trying to buy the properties just before they are sold on the courthouse steps?

Occasionally, when sellers reach the eleventh hour and acknowledge the fact that they are going to lose their property and get nothing if they let it go to a foreclosure sale, they will be willing to make a favorable deal. If you can give them a little money, you may be able to get some good deals, but you have to be very careful. There may well be second or third mortgages or other liens against the property that a foreclosure will wipe out, so if you are able to make a deal with the seller prior to foreclosure, as we mentioned in an earlier question, be sure to get a thorough title search and title insurance at the closing.

We've heard that cash is king when buying real estate. Is this also true when buying REOs from banks?

How to Find the Ideal Seller

It is especially true when buying REO from banks. Once banks foreclose, it usually leaves them with a bit of a bad taste for the properties. For this reason banks will be much more flexible on price if they know they can get rid of the properties without having to make "loans to facilitate" to dispose of them. Even if you have to borrow the money, if you borrow it from another bank and pay cash to the bank that foreclosed, you often can get some really good deals.

PART IV

How to Power Negotiate

We included an entire section on negotiating in *The Weekend Millionaire's Secrets to Investing in Real Estate* because we believe that your ability to make a good deal depends on your ability to negotiate well. "You'll never make money faster than you will when you're negotiating!" A member of Roger's golf club once was listed in the *Guinness Book of World Records* as the highest-paid heart surgeon in the world, but even he agrees that he makes more money per hour when he's negotiating his business deals.

In this part we will address many of your questions about negotiating and give you some additional tips that we were unable to include in the limited section on negotiating. Throughout your investing career, you will be negotiating constantly. Don't let the thought of having to negotiate make you become nervous and afraid. Once you understand that negotiating is a learnable skill just as much as finance or any other part of becoming a successful investor, you will learn that it is not only fun but also can be very rewarding.

17

Profit Is Made When You Buy

We stressed that the money is made when you buy, not when you sell, for two reasons. First, if you follow the Weekend Millionaire program, you're never going to sell. Mike owns hundreds of properties and has never sold one. Buy right, and the income will flow. Your working capital comes from refinancing your properties. You don't have to pay income taxes on the money you receive. You can even deduct the interest on your federal income tax return (if it's your residence, you're limited to the cost of the home plus the cost of the improvements). You don't even have to pay Social Security taxes on it!

Second, if you were to sell a property, you only would be able to sell it for the market value. You can't sell a property for more than it's worth any more than you can sell stock for more than it's listed.

Is land a good investment? I've got a chance to buy some land for a few hundred an acre. It's in the middle of nowhere, but the value of land always goes up, doesn't it?

Profit Is Made When You Buy

We don't think that land is an investment. It's more of a speculation. It's not as good as rental houses for several reasons: First, it doesn't generate income. Perhaps you can get a rancher to graze cattle on it, but it's never going to cover the cost of owning it. Second, you'll probably have to put at least 30 percent down to get a purchase loan on it. If you're buying from a developer, he or she might give you a low down payment but probably will require a higher interest rate. Third, when you sell, you probably won't be able to get your cash out because the buyer will expect you to carry back financing. You can make money on land, and Roger has made money on land, but it doesn't provide the solid investment potential that rental houses do. Most money is made in land using the "changing use changes value" theory. That theory says that if you can change the use of the land, you can increase the value dramatically. For example, we know an investor who has made a fortune buying large tracks of land, dividing them up into five-acre lots, and putting in landscaping, roads, and recreational areas. He changed the land from agricultural use to recreational use. If you could buy a residential lot in town and get it zoned for commercial use, you probably could make a good profit. But you need a lot of expertise and a lot of luck to make it happen. To answer your question, land can go down in value despite the fact that "they aren't making any more," as Will Rogers pointed out. And you still have to pay property taxes on it.

Is Phoenix [also asked about Palm Springs and Florida] a good market right now?

Phoenix is a hot market right now, but it has been a hot and cold market in the past. When you look at any community that primarily attracts vacationers, retirees, and people spending half a year in a warm climate, there are pluses and minuses. On the plus side, the climate is great, and population tends to grow. On the negative side, (1) there is ample land for expansion, so it's unlikely that scarcity will push up prices or rental values, (2) much of the work in the community is seasonal, which might make it difficult for you to find renters in the low-volume summer months and to be able to collect the rent if your tenants are laid off, and (3) prices can drop if the Canadian market softens. "Snowbirds," as we call them, can have a big impact on the economy. This could be because of a drop in the value of the

Canadian dollar or other factors. For example, the Palm Springs market tanked after the attack on the World Trade Center on 9/11 because Canadians were scared to come here. Also, we still recommend buying within close proximity of your home so that you can keep an eye on your properties.

You recommend using a property manager, so what's wrong with buying property in a distant town?

We get this question a lot, so our advice must seem contradictory. Even though you will have a property manager collect the rent for you and handle tenant requests, you will feel a lot more comfortable if you are able to drive by the property once in a while to keep an eye on it. You may spot deferred maintenance that the tenant and manager were reluctant to tell you about. You'll get a feel for whether or not the tenants are taking care of your property. Are weeds growing in the lawn? Are there broken-down cars everywhere? Also, you need to inspect the work of the property manager. Roger remembers a 36-unit apartment building he owned where he always seemed to have two or three vacancies—until he went to inspect the property. Then his resident manager told him that he had just filled the building the day before. It became clear that he was failing to show the units as rented until Roger came to inspect the books, and he was pocketing the rent.

Are there any other reasons that we shouldn't buy out of state?

Yes, it's far harder to judge values on out-of-state property. Texas property, for example, looks like a terrific bargain if you're from the Northeast or West Coast. But it doesn't mean anything to a smart investor. What matters is the purchase price versus the rental income that it will generate. Also, state laws may be different. A lot of California investors got hurt buying in Texas because in Texas you have personal liability for loans, whereas in California the property is all that you can lose.

I own five rental houses, and things are going well. Should I buy more houses or move up to apartment buildings?

We advise that your portfolio of real estate eventually should include both houses and apartment buildings. Apartment buildings typically offer a higher cash flow than houses because the ratio between the purchase cost and the rental income is more favorable to the owner. However, owning homes offers the advantage of easier-to-get loans and lower-rate financing. Also, if you should want to sell, single-family homes are easier to sell, so they offer you the advantage of liquidity. Just be cautious. Don't have too high a percentage of your investments in one property. If you have too many of your eggs in one basket, you're vulnerable to a downturn in the market for that kind of property or that neighborhood. With five houses in your portfolio, we think you're probably ready to start looking for a small two- to four-unit multifamily investment.

You mentioned Florida land in the early days being for trading and not for owning. Is that still going on?

Yes, irrational exuberance is certainly not confined to the stock market. We're reminded of what Will Rogers said about the California land boom: "It's the greatest game I ever saw. You can't lose. Everybody buys to sell and nobody buys to keep. What's worrying me is who is going to be the last owner. It's just like an auction; the only one stuck is the last one." The market that comes to mind today is the condominium boom in Miami. Investors hoping to resell at a profit are buying 75 percent of them. You don't need to be a mathematical genius to know that that's not going to work. Somebody's going to lose a lot of money. Yes, a few people are going to make money, but like Will Rogers' last owner, somebody's going to lose. Almost nobody gets hurt buying "bread and butter" rental properties the way we recommend.

18

Negotiating Pressure Points

As we stressed in an earlier chapter, you cannot make money investing in real estate by buying at retail prices any more than you could by opening a shoe store and expecting to make a profit when you buy your inventory at retail. You're looking for sellers who are under pressure to sell. In Chapter 18 of *The Weekend Millionaire's Secrets to Investing in Real Estate* we covered the three major pressure points: time pressure, information power, and projecting that you're prepared to walk away.

We got several questions about this from reluctant negotiators.

You say that the best buys come from people who desperately need to sell. If I did that, I would feel that I was taking advantage of people's misfortune. Don't you agree with me on that?

We totally disagree with that. The real estate market is open and fair. Every day hundreds of thousands of properties are sold, and every buyer thought that he or she got a good deal, and every seller thought that he or she got a good deal. While Mike, with his buy-and-hold philosophy, has never sold a property, Roger has sold dozens of properties. He recalls one that he sold at way below market value because it enabled him to put together an even better deal. He even gave away a piece of land once. He's glad that the buyers didn't refuse to buy from him because they thought they were taking advantage of him!

I don't like the idea of arguing with sellers about what their property is worth. Isn't there some way to avoid this unpleasantness?

We don't argue with sellers. We tell them what the property is worth to us. We explain why and how we came up with that figure. We tell them that we hope someone will pay them more, but if it doesn't happen, give us a call. Nobody's arguing. You probably feel that way because you're conflict-averse. You don't relish the idea of doing battle. You're a lover, not a fighter. There are people out there who love conflict. They're thinking, "I can't wait to get out there tonight, present this low offer, and watch the seller's response." You're probably not that way. If you'll realize that you're probably conflict-averse, you'll understand that you can be a much tougher negotiator without having to upset anybody.

I'm afraid that the sellers will laugh at me if I make a low offer. How do I deal with this?

Any offer is a good offer to a seller who hasn't had any offers. You just don't know until you present it. Roger once had a property listed with a broker at $219,000 and didn't get a single offer during the six-month listing. The real estate agent said, "We did get one offer at $179,000, but of course, we turned that down without consulting you." Why? Roger's reaction was that he had a buyer willing to pay $179,000. That's a lot of money. At least he would have liked the opportunity to meet the person and see what he could get him or her to do.

You say that time pressure will make it more likely that the buyer will accept your offer. You also say that if a seller won't accept an offer, tell him to call you if he changes his mind. Wouldn't it be better to put time pressure on the seller and tell him to "take it or leave it"?

This addresses the underlying question of who has the power in a negotiation. Your power is in direct relationship to the options that you have versus the options the seller has. If the seller has few or no options, by all means put some pressure on and get a decision right away. If the seller feels that waiting a week or two will enable him to develop more offers and therefore more options, you may do better to wait and make your move when the seller realizes that he's exhausted his options.

The property I'm looking at is listed with a broker. I think I can get a better deal if the listing has expired and the seller doesn't have to pay the broker. How can I find out when the listing expires?

Ask the seller or the broker! Reread the section on the value of asking tough questions (page 99 in *The Weekend Millionaire's Secrets to Investing in Real Estate*). Here's a little exercise that Mike's son Jason uses at his seminars. Find two people, and place a marble in one of the hands of one person. Have that person clench his or her fist tightly around the marble. Tell the other person to do whatever he or she can to get the marble from the first person. You'll watch that person struggle, plead, and finally beg the other person. Seldom will the person just say, "Will you give me your marble?" There's another issue here. You think that you will get a better buy because the seller doesn't have to pay a commission. Think this through a little. The property has been on the market for six months. It hasn't sold. We don't think you're getting a terrific buy just because the seller reduces the price by the amount of the broker's commission! That would only be a reduction of 6 percent from a price that didn't attract any buyers.

19

Win-Win Negotiating

Win-win negotiating depends on your ability to see the negotiation from the other person's point of view. Realize that other people don't necessarily want what you would want. You have to look at it from their point of view. This means that you must spend time gathering information about the sellers and using your people skills to convince them that you're not there to take advantage of them.

We get a lot of questions about what to do when the buyer and seller are far apart on price.

What's the best response when an offer is rejected with no counter?

When they refuse to counter, we recommend waiting a couple of weeks and calling them up again. There's a thing called "acceptance time" in negotiating skills. It takes people a while to realize that they're not going to get everything they want from the sale of their property. Most sellers have unreasonable expectations when they first put their property up for sale, particularly if it's their home. People develop a lot of emotional attachment to their home, and they unconsciously factor that into the price. As a real estate broker in California, Roger would teach his agents to start breaking this emotional attachment by referring to their home as a house or the property. In real estate sales jargon, buyers buy "homes," but sellers sell "houses." The other reason sellers inflate the perceived value of their property is that they confuse asking prices with actual selling prices. It's easy for them to find out what sellers in their neighborhood are asking for their property. It's much harder to find out what they actually sold for, which may be much less, but sellers hate to admit it.

I look at the prices houses are listed for and try to run the numbers like you taught in your book, and I can never come close to the asking price. How can I generate cash flow at these prices?

Real estate agents frequently list a property for more than it's worth, knowing that they can get price reductions from the seller later. When sellers decide to sell, they usually interview several real estate agents before they decide with whom to list. Thus the agents are competing against each other to get the listing. Very often sellers will go with the agent who tells them they can get them the most for their property. It's a terrible way to decide because they end up going with the biggest liar, but this is often what happens. A month later the listing agent will be asking them for a price reduction, but they still control the listing. Wait and watch the listing. When the first price reduction comes, the sellers will be a lot more flexible.

Any tips on how to negotiate deals that work when asking prices make it seem impossible or at least improbable to break even or generate cash flow?

We think that it's a good idea to put in writing why you are offering what you are. Sellers hate to think that you're low-balling them. Give them the reasons, such as what it's going to cost to rehab the property and get it rented, etc. "I realize that you're asking $200,000 for the property, but to get good renters, it will cost me $1,500 to replace the carpeting in the living room, $600 for a new washer and dryer, etc." Sellers are far less offended by low offers when you explain your reasoning. One negotiating technique that we use with good results is to make two offers at the same time, one for cash at a low price and one asking for favorable terms at the asking price or slightly above. The response of the sellers to these two offers tells us whether getting cash in hand is more important to the sellers or whether getting a monthly annuity is more attractive. Depending on which one gets a response, it tells us which way to go with future counteroffers.

How do you know when to stop negotiating and agree to the deal?

Here's where bracketing becomes so important. Bracketing tells you to assume that the negotiations will end up midway between the two opening negotiating positions. The seller is asking $200,000. You have figured the net operating income (NOI) and know that you can make the property work at $180,000, so you offer $160,000. We have a tremendous sense of fair play in this country. We tend to assume that if both sides give equally, then it's fair. Thus, when you finally agree on $180,000, it seems fair to the seller because you conceded as much as he or she did. When you reach this point, you know that it's time to stop negotiating and agree to the deal.

What about buying from heirs? I found a good property that needs fixing up. I offered the heirs 20 grand less than they asked. They met me halfway . . . still not low enough. I'm stumped on how to make the deal work. I can't figure out what they want from it. What should I do?

It sounds as though you need to learn a lot more about the people involved (the answer is always with the people and never with the property). Which of the relatives has a stake in this? Who wants to cash out, and who wants to hold on? What are they going to do with the money generated from the sale? Inherited property often produces some strange emotions. The more you can find out, the better you will do. Here are a couple of quick tips about gathering information: First, don't be afraid to ask the tough questions. Even if they refuse to answer, you're still gathering information. Second, try to get them out of the work environment. Information flows much more freely away from their office. If you can get them out to dinner or a game of golf, that's terrific, but even if you can just get them across the street to McDonald's for a cup of coffee, sellers are much more likely to share information with you. This is also a terrific opportunity for you to use the "terms versus price" tradeoff gambit. Try offering to agree to the $10,000 reduction, but only if they'll carry back financing at a favorable rate. A friend of ours found an interesting way to deal with heirs. He bought out one of the heirs' *rights* for the property. Then he became one of the "sellers." Now he was in a position where all other heirs have to deal with him. It was a risky move because he didn't control the property, but after a few weeks, the other heirs sold their shares to him.

There are two real estate agents between them and me. They won't let me talk to the seller. How do I get around this?

This means that you're dealing with a selling broker who is the subagent of the listing agent. This can happen when the selling agent has brought the property to your attention. However, if you're calling on an ad or responding to an open house, we suggest that you ask for the listing agent. This is the agent who knows the seller best and knows his or her needs. Another reason is that if the agent is getting both sides of the commission, he or she may be far more willing to give up some of it to make the deal work. We suggest that you challenge the agent to get the offer accepted by saying, "If you can't get it accepted, I want to reserve the right to meet with the seller and discuss the offer with him or her." Agents hate letting the buyer talk to the seller. They've all had experiences where the buyer looks at a home and offends the seller by saying, "We could really make this look nice." When you challenge agents like this, they work much harder to get the offer accepted.

My real estate agent quit. He sent me an e-mail saying he doesn't want to work with investors anymore. What should I do?

Some real estate agents love to negotiate, and some hate it. Much of it has to do with personality. Some people love a good fight, and some people hate adversity. Some people have a low tolerance for ambiguity and won't go into a situation where they don't know how it's going to turn out. Accountants and engineers tend to be that way. Some people love to go into tough situations where they don't know how it's going to turn out and battle for the best deal. Keep interviewing agents until you find one who loves to negotiate and gets a thrill out of presenting low offers.

Win-Win Negotiating

I found a run-down property, but the sellers won't come down to a price that will make it work for me using the Weekend Millionaire format. Now I don't know where to start. I really think I can turn that house into a jewel. What should I do?

Calculate what you would pay per month if the sellers took your cash offer; then calculate what interest rate they would have to give you on all or a portion of the financing to stay below that amount if you give them their asking price. By getting the sellers to carry back financing at less than market rate, you can get your monthly outlay down low enough that the rent will cover it.

There is a house in a good area that is for sale by the owner. The owner owns it free and clear. I made an offer with 10 percent down and asked the owner to carry back the balance secured by a first mortgage. She turned it down because she wants more cash than that. What should I do?

You get a first mortgage from a bank or mortgage broker, and the seller carries back a second. You can do even better if you find a private lender to make the first. Many individuals these days own CDs that are only paying them 2 to 3 percent. They would be happy to loan to you at 5 percent as long as the loan is secured by real estate.

How do I find someone who would take a chance on real estate loans instead of CDs?

Do you have friends, relatives, or acquaintances who have some money, especially older people who are looking for the income from their investments on which to live? They are all good sources. Also, you could run an ad in the newspaper offering x percent for a mortgage loan, etc.

My wife and I have been working hard to get our credit straight. It's been a long road. We've finally got the numbers right but still find it hard to overcome the past. How can we improve our credit rating?

Building great credit takes time. There aren't really any valid shortcuts. You need to commit to making your payments on time so that the favorable items on your credit report swamp the negatives. The key is to not backslide once you get on the right road. Certainly you should get your credit reports from the three major credit reporting companies and challenge any errors. Don't believe people or companies that say they can clean up your credit. They can't. Only challenge items that are genuine errors or where adding an explanation might help.

It eats me up that we have equity in our house that we could use to buy a rental house . . . but can't touch it. I've tried to get an equity loan, but the banks won't approve it. I don't make enough income by myself, and my wife has some negatives on her credit report. My number is around 700. My wife's number is around 660, so we can't get the loan together. How can I get them to make me a loan?

Keep fixing your financial problems by paying off credit cards and making your payments on time. Then you will be able to get a home-equity loan. Get your scores to 720 or above, and you'll be fine. Our advice is to get the credit straightened out first. Right now you're in danger of being able to get a home-equity loan for the down payment on the rental but not being able to get financing to buy the rental. Buying with marginal credit often can be as dangerous as erecting a building on a shaky foundation.

I'm having trouble finding properties where I can make the figures work. Should I take a chance on negative cash flow, hoping that I can get the rents up enough?

You can get rich buying the right properties, but you can just as easily go broke buying the wrong ones. Don't force the issue. Make offers that work, and be patient. Eventually, one of them will be accepted.

I've bought my first rental, and the cash flow is beginning to build. I am so eager to get my second rental that I can't stand still. Did you feel this way when you were getting started?

Don't get too eager. In *The Weekend Millionaire's Secrets to Investing in Real Estate* we list the biggest mistakes that real estate investors make. Mistake number 1 in the last chapter of the book is *being impatient*!

Win-Win Negotiating

Do you have a book on negotiation that is specific for the real estate investor? Or is that the Weekend Millionaire *book?*

Mike has used Roger's *Secrets of Power Negotiating* audio program for 20 years and made millions with the techniques and tactics he teaches. *The Weekend Millionaire's Secrets to Real Estate Investing* gives a good overview of negotiating techniques as they apply to buying (not selling) real estate. There is far more detail in Roger's book *Secrets of Power Negotiating*, second edition (Career Press, 2000). We do plan to do a real estate investors negotiating book as part of the *Weekend Millionaire* series of books.

20

Beginning Negotiating Gambits

There are many similarities between negotiating and the game of chess. They are both played by a set of rules. Learning the moves may take only a couple of hours. Knowing when to use the moves may take a lifetime. We divided the negotiating gambits into terms that a chess player would understand: beginning gambits, middle gambits, and ending gambits. To a chess player, the word "gambit" implies risk—you put that pawn out there, and you might lose it.

Here are some questions we received about the "beginning gambits"— the things you do in the early stages of the negotiation to be sure that you're setting it up for a successful conclusion.

Here's a negotiating question for you. How do you bracket the offer when the seller won't tell you how much he or she wants for the property?

It's hard to get a good buy from someone who is not motivated to sell. You've got to spend some time with the seller and discover his or her motivations. What would the seller do with the money if he or she did sell?

Would the seller like to turn his or her equity into an annuity for his or her retirement years? Would the seller like to move to a warmer climate? If the seller doesn't have any motivation, you need to create some. Wouldn't you love to live closer to your grandchildren? Ever thought of retiring to a beach home in Hawaii, where you could walk barefoot on the warm sand every morning? Did you ever dream of buying a sailboat and escaping to Tahiti? Is the seller buying a condo in Florida? Make the seller smell the sea breezes blowing across the patio. Get the seller to taste the salt on his or her margarita! Remember the story we told in *The Weekend Millionaire's Secrets to Investing in Real Estate* of the old man in Seattle who didn't want to sell his land until the developer offered to name the shopping center after him?

I have a question on the "You'll have to do better than that" gambit. How do you respond when the seller says, "How much better do I have to do?"

You're referring to the "vise" gambit. We get the seller to state his or her price. We consider it carefully, and then we say, "You'll have to do better than that!" If they respond with, "How much better than that do I have to do?" trying to get you to commit to a specific, then this is when we'd go to the "higher authority" gambit: "I've got to sell this to my partners. Give me a number so that I will have a chance of selling this deal to them."

Your one gambit about asking what is the least you would take for a property saved me $12,000. These negotiating skills are great. Do you have any other suggestions?

Another negotiating tactic we use frequently is to ask for several things that we don't expect to get—things such as furniture, paintings, all the closing costs, etc. When we concede those items, the seller feels that he or she has won. Another gambit is the "red herring" gambit. You make a big deal out of an issue about which you don't care and then trade it off for an issue about which you do care. Perhaps you make a big issue out of having the seller carry back financing when you know that he or she doesn't want to do that. Then you can say, "How much will you take off the price if I get a new loan and pay cash?"

I called a broker who specializes in investment property. He started to talk to me about CAP rates. I was too embarrassed to tell him that I didn't know what he was talking about. What's a CAP rate? Is it the most you would pay for a property?

No, CAP is short for "capitalization." It projects what your return on investment would be if you paid cash for the property. This enables a serious investor to compare the return on investment to buying gold or stocks and bonds. To calculate it, you take the gross rental income after projected vacancies and deduct the expenses—the same expenses that we teach you to deduct when figuring net operating income (NOI): maintenance, insurance, taxes, utilities, and management costs. Then divide what's left by the purchase price to get the CAP rate. You'll end up with a number like .09, which means that if you paid cash for the building, you'd get a 9 percent return on your money. We don't pay much attention to CAP rates because they assume a cash purchase, which nobody would do because you surrender the big advantage of leverage. Thus CAP rates are only useful if you want to compare similar properties. Far more important is the terms of financing. This is the big expense, and it's the big opportunity to tailor the financing so that it's a win for both parties.

I'm having trouble figuring out what a property is worth. Is there some kind of formula for working that out? Does it help to know what the seller paid for the property?

Let's start out with the classic definition of "value." A property is worth what a willing buyer will pay and a willing seller will accept when both are informed and neither one is under pressure. "Willing" means that the seller wants to sell and the buyer wants to buy. "Informed" means that they've done enough research to know what the property should sell for, meaning that they've hired an appraiser or they've researched comparable sales in the area. "Not under pressure" means that the seller is not in financial trouble or has not just been transferred and needs to sell quickly, and the buyer is not under pressure to invest funds so that he or she can defer taxes or has not just been transferred and must find a place quickly. Note that nowhere in this does it talk about how much the seller paid for the property. The seller could have been given the property, and it wouldn't affect the value. From a negotiating standpoint, any information such as this is helpful but it doesn't affect value.

Beginning Negotiating Gambits

The sellers say that they have an appraisal on their property and that is what the property's worth and what I should pay them. How accurate is an appraisal?

In our experience, appraisals can vary widely depending on the experience and integrity of the appraiser and who's paying for the appraisal and why. Roger remembers selling a property where the buyers had agreed to a high price but he needed an equally high appraisal so that the buyers could get financing. He met the appraiser at the property and gave him a bottle of scotch and a list of comparable properties that had sold for high prices. He drove him to the comparables and did everything he could to build rapport and make the appraiser's job easy for him. The appraisal came in 20 percent higher than even the high price at which the property had sold. On another occasion Roger was refinancing a property but only asking for a 50 percent loan-to-value loan. The bank-appointed appraiser knew this and gave an appraisal that was enough to get the loan but still was 20 percent less than the property was really worth. Even appraisers will tell you that an appraisal is nothing more than one person's opinion of what the property is worth on that particular day.

How do appraisers come up with a price?

Most appraisals are made by the comparison method. The appraiser finds out what properties in the neighborhood sold for and comes up with a value based on that. If the home is in a tract of homes that are all basically the same, it's a simple matter. If the market has gone up or down since the sale, the appraiser just needs to adjust the appraisal price for that factor. Appraisers usually specialize in a particular area, so they get to know all the homes. After a while, they develop a file on nearly all the properties in an area, so they can pull out an appraisal from the last time they appraised it. If the property is not in a conforming area, it gets more complicated. The appraiser will add or subtract for the features of the comparables versus the subject property. The subject property has 500 more square feet than the comparable property, so add $10,000. The comparable property has a swimming pool that the subject property doesn't, so deduct $8,000, and so on. If there are no comparables, the appraiser uses the reproduction method. It's rarely used and usually only on nonconforming properties such as churches and commercial properties. The appraiser puts a value on the land using the comparison method and then calculates what it would cost to reproduce the building today. Then the appraiser depreciates the value of the building (not the land) based on its useful life and age. Note that the Weekend Millionaire method of valuing properties doesn't use either of these methods. We are only interested in the rental income that the property will generate. If the rental income will support the cost of owning the property, it's a good buy. If it will generate excess cash flow, it's an even better buy.

What do I do if the sellers have read your book too and know about your tactics?

Don't worry about it. We think that you're much better off to be negotiating with someone who knows how to negotiate. It's when one side doesn't know how to negotiate that you have problems. This is when the picket signs go up outside. A classic example of this is an employee asking his or her boss for a raise in pay. The boss doesn't want to lose the employee but needs to curtail the demand, so he or she says, "That will be hard to get approved right now." Instead of starting a productive negotiation where both sides could win, the employee quits, and everybody loses. Look for Roger's book, *Secrets of Power Salary Negotiations* (Career Press, 2006). When the sellers don't know how to negotiate, they get upset at your first offer. We much prefer to deal with someone who knows how to negotiate.

What do I do if the sellers flinch at my offer?

This is a good sign because it means that they know how to negotiate! Just laugh and say, "That was a terrific flinch! Where did you learn how to do that? Have you been reading *The Weekend Millionaire*?"

I don't expect the sellers to accept my first offer, but how do I know when it's a waste of time and when it's worth spending more time on it?

Negotiators talk about the "likely settlement range." This is when both sides' negotiating ranges overlap. Let's say that the seller is asking $200,000 but might take $170,000 if nothing better comes along. You're offering $160,000 but could still make it work at $175,000. This means that the sellers' and buyers' negotiating ranges overlap between $170,000 and $175,000. Negotiators call this the "likely settlement range." Neophyte investors would tend to think, "We're $40,000 apart. I don't think the seller will come down that much." Maybe not, but when you think that the buyer also may be able to come up in price, it makes the deal look that much more doable—particularly if the seller is willing to do some creative financing or the real estate agent is flexible about his or her commission.

Should I ask the real estate agent to reduce his or her commission?

This is a touchy subject! Roger is a real estate broker and doesn't want to get excommunicated by the National Association of Realtors for suggesting it, but it happens. We think that a good real estate agent earns his or her money and shouldn't have to cut his or her fee, but look at it realistically. If the property is selling for $200,000 and the listing broker is charging 6 percent, there is a fee of $12,000 involved. The listing broker gets half of this, and the selling broker (representing the buyer) gets the other half. Each shares it with the agent at their agreed-on commission split, which might range from 50 to 80 percent. There's some serious money involved here, and if the agents can kick in a little of their commission to make a deal work that otherwise wouldn't, this is great, and they've been known to do it. Even just asking an agent to carry back his or her commission in a note, rather than cash, may be enough to swing the deal. The chances of this happening are greatly increased if the agent is getting both sides of the deal. This is why we recommend dealing with the listing agent if you can. The listing agent knows the seller better and has a bigger stake in putting the deal together. He or she may be more protective of the seller, but we still think it's the way to go. Realize that asking an agent to cut his or her commission may be penny wise and pound foolish. Your long-term goal is to build relationships with agents to encourage them to bring you good deals in the future.

I get confused by the relationship of the buyers' and sellers' agents. Just who is working for whom?

This is in a state of flux right now. It used to be very clear. The listing broker was employed by the seller to find a buyer. The selling broker was a subagent of the listing broker, so all the agents were being paid by the seller, and there was a fiduciary relationship between both listing and selling brokers and the seller. If you were a buyer, your agent (called the "selling agent"—confusing isn't it?) would tell you, "Don't tell me anything that you wouldn't want the seller to know because I'm technically working for the seller." This system worked well for decades until the trial lawyers got hold of it. If the buyer was suing the seller because something went wrong with the property, the lawyer would sue the selling broker also because he or she technically was working for the seller. This led to a shift in thinking and a move to buyer's agency. In many states the selling broker separates himself or herself from the seller by declaring in writing that he or she is representing the buyer even though he or she is being paid by the seller. As negotiators, we like this. The battle lines are drawn more clearly, and buyers and sellers both understand better who is working for whom. In practice, it works differently. The truth is that each party is working for themselves. The agents want to close the deal by any ethical means they can muster. The sellers want to get the best deal for themselves, and the buyers want the best deal they can cut by any ethical means. This is what makes negotiating so much fun!

What's a buyer's agent? There's an agent in town who wants me to pay him for finding the property. Is this a good idea?

A buyer's agent is different from the buyer's agency we just described. Buyer's agents are a minority, but they are out there. They work strictly for the buyer. This is more popular in commercial real estate, where a chain restaurant or store employs an agent to find potential locations in a community. The way that the buyer's agent gets paid is totally up to negotiation. You may have to pay such an agent a retainer. You may pay him or her a commission when you buy a property. The seller typically will reduce the selling price because he or she is paying only the listing broker. Or sometimes the seller pays the agent directly, with the clear understanding that the agent only represent the buyer. Our opinion? We think that nothing beats getting out there and looking for the properties yourself. You learn the market better and become skilled at recognizing a good deal when one pops up.

21

Middle Negotiating Gambits

As the negotiation progresses, other factors come in to play. The middle negotiating gambits are designed to keep the momentum building toward a successful conclusion. Having a vague "higher authority" is a great way to put pressure on the seller without being confrontational. Not offering to split the difference helps to make the seller feel that he or she won. The "tradeoff" gambit teaches you never to make a concession to the other side unless you get something in return.

The questions we received on this topic covered a wide range.

You recommend buying business cards and passing them around to attract sellers. As an individual investor, should I put my name on the cards, or should I also make up a company name to make it look more impressive?

We've always just used our names. Our attitude is that the more impressive the name of the entity, the more likely you are to get scammed. "Worldwide Real Estate Investors" may sound grand, but we're more inclined to trust

"John Doe—Real Estate Investor." Also, we see a negotiating disadvantage in using a grand name. John Doe may have a legitimate reason to require the sellers to come down another $1,000, but why is Worldwide Real Estate Investors getting so hot under the collar?

What's a DBA, and do I need one?

Some people prefer not to have their name on their business. The simplest way to do this is to create a DBA, which stands for "doing business as," e.g., John Doe, DBA Main Street Properties. The reason you need to file a DBA is that banks won't give you a checking account under your business name unless you create one. It means filing a DBA in the county in which you do business. You must publish your intention to do so in a general-circulation newspaper so that the actual ownership of the company is a matter of public record. The easiest way to do this is to do an Internet search for DBA in your county. You'll find companies that perform this service for you. After it has been published and recorded, take your papers to your bank and open up your checking account.

In the "higher authority" gambit you suggest deferring the decision to buy to another party, such as a partner, committee, or board. The bottom line is that I am going to buy the property. At the closing, it'll be my name alone on the legal documents, not a company, committee, or partners. They'll know that I lied during the negotiation when they see that I'm taking title as an individual. How do you pull this off without losing credibility with the professionals involved in the sale?

Our cards give our name, contact information, and state that we're real estate investors, but this doesn't prevent us from using our attorney, accountants, bankers, family, and potential partners in new ventures as higher authorities. Higher authority is a terrific way to put pressure on the other side without confrontation. "I wish I could go along with that, but my accountants would have a fit!" Remember to make sure that your higher authority is a vague entity, such as partners or bankers, not an individual. If you use an individual, the sellers may want to go around you and deal directly with the higher authority.

I don't think that my bank will lend to a DBA or a small corporation. How should I take title to the property?

The only people who care how you take title are the ones who are lending you the money. Unless you're a publicly traded corporation, they are going to want you to personally sign for the loan. Thus you can take title any way you want as long as you personally sign for the loan. You may want to consider taking title as a single-member limited liability corporation (LLC). This is a business entity that can have a very important-sounding name, but it can use your Social Security number as its tax ID number, and properties held in its name are treated the same on your tax return as if you owned them in your individual name. Most banks will work with you on this, especially if you let them know that you want to hold the properties this way for estate-planning purposes. Discuss this possibility with your bankers and with legal and tax advisors for more information.

What's wrong with offering to split the difference? Very often the other side will agree to it, and you're all done. Why waste time negotiating if you can reach agreement simply?

We think that it's important to make the seller feel that he or she won in the initial negotiation. Let's say that the seller is asking $200,000 and you're offering $195,000. You know that if you said, "Let's split the difference," the seller would agree to it. In reality, what you've done is propose $197,500, and you're trying to make the seller agree to your proposal. If you could get the seller to offer to split the difference, now he or she has proposed $197,500, and you are reluctantly agreeing to the seller's proposal. This may seem like a subtle thing to you, but it's very significant in terms of making the seller feel that he or she has won. Realize that about 20 percent of all real estate deals fall through between the time the sellers and buyers sign the contract and the deal is closed. Half a dozen little things come up that need to be resolved. If the sellers felt that they won in the initial negotiation, they'll be more likely to overlook those things. If they felt that they lost, then every step of the way they're looking for ways to recoup the ground they felt they lost.

*In the "trading off" gambit you talk about asking for a reciprocal conces-
sion anytime the other side asks you for a concession. You suggest saying,
"If we can do that for you, 'What can you do for me?'" Wouldn't I be better
off to ask for something specific?*

We don't think so—for two reasons. First, it's confrontational. When you say
to a seller, "If you want me to delay the closing for a week, I expect you to
pay me rent," it sets up a confrontational tone to the negotiation. Remember that in that final week before closing, everyone is uptight. The sellers
may be leaving a home where they raised their children. They may be having second thoughts about selling at all. The buyer still may be worried
about getting the loan approved or raising the cash for the down payment.
It's better not to create any confrontation. Second, we think that you'll get
more with an open request than you will if you ask for something specific.
You always can revert to asking for something specific. Let's say that the
seller says to you, "There's nothing more we can do for you. We gave you the
best deal in the world." You can now respond with, "The problem is that I'm
going to have a tough time getting my partners to go along with this. You
have to give me something to help me sell them with. How about allowing
us to show the property to prospective tenants during that final week? Does
that seem fair to you?"

*I live in a small town, and everyone knows who I am. I don't think that I
can use the "higher authority" gambit, can I?*

Sure, you can. Your "higher authority" becomes the entity to whom you
have delegated authority. This is one of the things that make using property
managers so effective. The property manager can say to the tenants, "The
owners of this property won't allow me to let the rent go in arrears. If you
don't pay by the fifth of the month, I have to file an eviction notice." The
owner can say, "My property managers won't allow me to make decisions
like that. They insist that it's their job."

22

Ending Negotiating Gambits

Using the ending negotiating gambits is critical to successful conclusion of the negotiation. Tension builds, and both sides can be volatile. You will sense this in the questions that we were asked. Like a horse race that is won only at the finish line, no negotiation is successful unless agreement is reached.

I'm in a tough negotiation to buy a rental house that was a "For Sale by Owner." Several little things have caused the sellers to get upset with me. Now the owner's wife is saying that her husband is so upset about this that he won't even talk to me anymore. Any suggestions?

It sounds to us as though they're playing "good guy/bad guy" with you. Roger ran into this a lot when he was president of a large real estate company in California. He would get the problems when the salesperson couldn't handle them, the office manager couldn't handle them, and the regional manager couldn't handle them. By that time the buyers and sellers were so hot that it was difficult to get them to talk. We suggest that you try to go around the wife and talk to the husband directly. Perhaps you can call him at work or on his cell phone. We suspect that you'll find that he's a pussy-cat. The wife doesn't want you talking to him because she knows he'll go along with anything. Buying directly from a "For Sale by Owner" puts the negotiation in a different context. Remember that real estate agents are taught never to let the buyer talk to the seller. There's just too much danger of emotions getting in the way.

I've read what you teach about nibbling, but I feel that I'm getting gnashed on! Ever since I started this purchase, the sellers have been coming back to me for small concessions. It wasn't enough to worry about at the start, but now the demands are growing, and it's threatening the entire deal. How can I stop them?

Remember what we taught you in Chapter 21 of *The Weekend Millionaire's Secrets to Investing in Real Estate* about trading off? Anytime you are asked for a concession in the negotiations, ask for something in return. Say, "If we can do that for you, what can you do for me." If they know that every time they ask you for something, you will ask for something in return, it stops them from constantly coming back for more.

I tried to get the sellers to carry back financing, but they wouldn't agree. We signed a deal where I would put 20 percent down, and they would get all cash. This will still work for me, but it would be a much sweeter deal if I could get them to carry back some of the financing. Is it too late to get them to change their mind?

Be aware that you're in sensitive territory. In America, when the deal is struck, it is considered the end of the negotiations. This is not so in all parts of the world. In some cultures, the signing of a contract denotes the *start* of the negotiations. In America, any attempt to change the deal is looked on with suspicion. You need to tread carefully, but this is where the principle of nibbling comes in. You can get things later in the negotiation that you can't get earlier. But you've got to frame it as a benefit to the sellers, not to you. Call the sellers and say, "I've been thinking about this transaction, and I think I've come up with a way to make this an even better deal for you. The way the deal is structured is fine with me, but if you were willing to carry back just 10 percent of the price, you would get a good return on your investment, and you'd save a lot of money on taxes." The theory of nibbling is that people fight a decision until they've made it, and then they subconsciously want to do things to reinforce the decision. Now that you have a relationship with the sellers and they have trusted you enough to sign a contract with you, you stand a better chance of getting them to go along with your suggestion to carry back financing.

I presented an offer to a seller, and he took a quick glance at it and tossed it back across the table, saying, "I've already turned down an offer for $5,000 more than that." It made sense to me. Why should he accept my offer when he's turned down better offers? I didn't know what to say, so I just picked up my offer and left, feeling stupid. What could I have done differently?

Remember that we taught you where power comes from in a negotiation. It comes from being able to convince the other side that you have more options than it does. When you're presenting an offer, you gain power by convincing the seller that you have all kinds of other properties available to you. Conversely, it's the seller's job to convince you that he or she has options. It is a convincing strategy for the seller to tell you that he has other people who will pay more. However, remember that negotiators don't deal in reality; they deal in perceptions. If you believe it to be true, it's true as far as that negotiation is concerned. Many sellers turn down offers and later regret it. Or perhaps he didn't tell you all the details of the offer. It may have been a no-money-down offer from people with bad credit. We find it hard to believe that if the buyer and seller were only $5,000 apart on price they couldn't have worked something out, so we're suspicious. Instead of walking away, you should have engaged the seller by saying, "Let me tell you how I came up with this price, and perhaps it will make more sense to you."

I presented an offer to a Chinese seller and asked him to make a decision right away, using time pressure as a tool. He turned me down, and later I heard he took less from another buyer. What did I do wrong?

With foreigners or people from foreign cultures, give them plenty of time to get to know you. Americans are what negotiators call "low context" negotiators, meaning that the context in which the contract was signed is not that important to us. We don't feel that we need to have a warm relationship with the other person because we have a contract that will hold up in court. Also, we have such a mobile society that we are used to dealing with strangers. Many other countries lack an effective civil justice system, so they place more reliance on knowing and trusting the other person. Take your time to get to know them, and allow trust to grow.

I signed a contract to buy a property from a Saudi, and then the seller tried to change the terms on me. I got so upset I demanded that he cancel the deal and give me my deposit back, which he did. What would you have done?

Realize that Americans view the contract as the end of the deal. When the hand is shaken, the deal is done. People from other cultures don't see it that way. We're not putting them down. They simply see it differently. In the Arab world, a contract means little more than a letter of intent does to us. It signals the start of the negotiations, not the end. In Korea, a contract is only good as long as the conditions in which the contract was signed stay the same. If conditions change, then neither side feels obligated to abide by the contract. When dealing with foreigners, our advice is to make it very clear that signing the contract means to you that no changes will be allowed.

23

You're Negotiating All the Time

In the final chapter of the negotiating section of *The Weekend Millionaire's Secrets to Investing in Real Estate* we pointed out that a real estate investor doesn't just negotiate with sellers. You negotiate with everyone. You negotiate with property managers, plumbers, painters, electricians, suppliers, and everyone else with whom you do business. Every penny that you take in and every penny that you spend involves a negotiation with someone. The better negotiator you become, the more successful investor you will be.

The fact that you're constantly negotiating triggered some additional questions in our readers' minds.

If I'm going to hire a property manager, won't he or she do all these negotiations for me? Why do I need to learn negotiating skills?

For one thing, you'll need to negotiate with your property manager. What will he or she charge you? How will he or she submit bills to you? When does he or she expect to get paid? What services does that cover? Then you'll need to teach your property manager how to negotiate with the people he or she engages. Some work may not be covered by your agreement with your property manager. If you're rehabbing a property to get it ready for renting, for example, you may be dealing directly with the contractors and suppliers yourself.

I'm afraid that if I beat a contractor down on price, he or she won't do as good a job. Isn't that a danger?

You should never hire a contractor based on price. Decide on the contractor that you want to do the work first. How much experience does he or she have? Can he or she give you good references from previous jobs? If he or she is not going to do the work himself or herself, will he or she use high-quality workers on the job? How much personal supervision will he or she give them? Someone who impresses you on all these criteria will not lower his or her standards just because you agreed on a lower price. Therefore, decide on the contractor that you want first, and then use your negotiating skills to get him or her to give you the best possible price.

How can I tell if a contractor is giving me a fair price?

Until you have enough experience to know what a job costs, you should get at least three quotes. Look for the contractor who takes careful measurements and takes time to figure out his or her costs. We never trust a contractor who takes a quick look at the problem and says, "It'll cost you $3,000." We've had some ridiculous quotes from contractors like this. They're just playing the numbers game. There are a percentage of property owners who don't know or care what it costs. The "quick quote" contractor is just trolling for suckers.

Do you prefer working with large contractors or family-owned businesses?

Be wary of contractors who take out full-page ads in the Yellow Pages. Often they are just sales agents for other contractors, and they're getting a big chunk off the top for booking the work. We're also wary of those huge plumbing companies that have big gleaming trucks all over the freeways. Sometimes their quotes are 10 times what a reputable family-owned plumbing business will charge. We'd much rather deal with a small local contractor who has been in business in the community for most of his or her life. We've found that if you can build a good working relationship with a small but reputable contractor, it can pay huge dividends in the long run.

Any tips for getting a good buy on a car for my business?

Car buying has changed a lot since the advent of the Internet. New car dealers used to tell us that they had to take buyers through 12 steps before they could close a sale. Now they tell us that buyers have already gone through the first eight steps on the Internet before they reach the showroom. They know what's available. They know what options they want, and they've picked out the color and upholstery from pictures on the manufacturer's Web site. They know what the car cost the dealer and what financing is available to them and what it will cost them. The biggest myth in car buying is that dealer cost is the best you can do. Dealers can sell to you at their cost and still make a very good profit because of volume incentives that the manufacturers give them. Leasing companies, who might want 20 cars or trucks, can buy at 4 percent below dealer cost, and the dealer is happy to have the business. Roger once filmed a television segment where the producer followed him into a Chevrolet dealership and filmed him buying a car. He was able to get it for 7 percent below dealer cost.

Should I buy from a local dealer so that I get better service?

It doesn't matter. Your local dealer will be happy to service your car even if you didn't buy it there. Warranty service is not absorbed by the dealer; it's charged back to the factory. Do your homework, get quotes from several dealers, and go with the lowest price.

What do you think about fixed-price dealers like Saturn?

We think that they are artificially maintaining their prices by limiting the supply. If they had 100,000 unsold cars sitting on a lot somewhere, they'd be eager to negotiate. General Motors once tested a "fair price" policy in California. The company lowered the sticker prices but wouldn't budge from that. Ford studied what GM was doing to see if it should adopt the same policy. Admittedly, Ford is not an impartial entity, but it found that people were paying 3 percent more to buy a car from a "fair price" dealer than a buyer who did even a fair job of negotiating with a regular dealer. Three percent on a car purchase is several hundred dollars. This is a good illustration of how Americans are reluctant to negotiate. Untrained negotiators would rather pay more money and not have the hassle.

I can't negotiate with a clerk in a department store, can I?

You can, but you have to do it within the parameters of the way the store does business. The store can't authorize its clerks to negotiate prices because they'd be giving their friends better deals. But stores do authorize their clerks to give discounts under certain conditions. These might include taking a floor model rather than a new one in a box, taking an item that has minor damage or is even dusty, taking an item that has been on sale recently or will be soon, and taking an item that another store is selling for less. The key is learning the store's policy. At the place where Roger parks his car at Los Angeles airport, he knows that if a customer is unhappy, the clerks are authorized to take one day's charge off the bill. He doesn't take advantage of it, but if the car is not ready when he gets there, he knows he can quickly get one day taken off the bill. He probably could get two days if he worked at it, but it's not worth the extra effort.

PART V

How to Structure the Offer

This section has produced hundreds of questions from readers. The chapters dealing with valuing properties, structuring and writing offers, how nothing-down deals work, and the tax advantages of owning real estate form the nucleus of the Weekend Millionaire method of investing in real estate, and people want to know more about it.

In *The Weekend Millionaire's Secrets to Investing in Real Estate,* we explained how a successful buy-and-hold strategy for real estate investing depends on your ability to buy properties at wholesale. We introduced the concept of ignoring price and looking for wholesale values. This is not a get-rich-quick scheme, and in order to grasp the concept one must understand the time value of money.

The Weekend Millionaire method relies on negotiating purchases that can be supported by the net operating income (NOI) properties will generate and then by allowing the passage of time to make you rich. You build equity through the combination of appreciation and debt reduction, while you generate cash flow with gradual increases in rent. The secret to early retirement is to add one property after another to your portfolio and watch your cash flow build from a trickle to a stream and eventually to a torrent of unearned income.

The key is patience and persistence. When you treat your growing collection of properties the way you would a 401(k) or IRA plan and leave them alone to grow and mature, eventually they produce enough unearned income to allow you to quit work and never have to worry about earning a living the rest of your life. This concept is clearly defined in our book *Weekend Millionaire Mindset: How Ordinary People Can Achieve Extraordinary Success*.

We encourage you to stick with the security of your day job and let it provide your daily living expenses while you invest a few hours of your spare time on the weekends to build real wealth. We want you to think of wealth a little differently. We realize that most people view wealth as how big a house you live in, how fancy a car you drive, how nice your clothes are, the country club to which you belong, and all the similar trappings that ordinary people associate with wealth. Our measure of wealth is not based on the standard of living you have, but rather by how long you can sustain that standard of living if you suddenly can't work and earn money. In other words, wealth is an income stream.

Now let's move on to the questions our readers have asked about this concept.

24

Valuing Single-Family Properties

Since valuing single-family properties has produced more questions than any other topic, this is a long chapter. Many of the questions we have received on this subject are just slightly different ways of asking the same question; so we have tried to consolidate similar questions into more general ones that cover the gist of the subject.

Given conventional thinking regarding bank financing and inexperience with unconventional financing, many people have a difficult time seeing the difference between price and value. No matter how many times we say that value is determined by the combination of price and terms (what you pay and how you pay it), we still get hundreds of questions about how to make the numbers work at today's prices.

We hope the questions that follow will give you a better perspective about the concept of value versus price and how it relates to valuing single-family properties.

How to Structure the Offer

What if the only way to get a positive cash flow is to have an interest-only loan? Is that a bad thing?

This may be necessary in markets where the ratio of rent to purchase price makes it difficult to achieve a cash flow. You will have no cash flow at first, but once you're able to raise the rents, cash will start to flow. We recommend that you refinance to an amortizing loan as soon as you're able so that you will start paying down the debt. The Weekend Millionaire program is a buy-and-hold program. You build wealth in three ways: from paying down the mortgage, from appreciation, and from raising the rents.

If you were going to flip the property, interest-only loans make more sense. Al Lee, a successful real estate investor from Dallas, told us this: "I have eight interest-only loans, and I think they are terrific. Why? Because of cash flow! If you pay interest only, you will get more cash in your pocket each month because your payment is lower. The heck with paying off the loan! I know you disagree, but I say let inflation pay down the loan for you. I have large business equity lines of credit that I can use for anything I want to use them for. What I do is use them to negotiate a cash purchase, draw enough additional cash from the line to get the property fixed up and rented, and then I look for term financing and repay the line so that I can use the money over again."

A mortgage broker set up an interest-only loan when I bought my new home and wanted to keep my old one for rental income. It made the numbers look best to go with an interest-only loan. I don't like not getting the house paid off, but it is giving me a $500 positive cash-flow without taxes and insurance factored in. Doesn't that make sense?

You could take a five-year interest-only loan now and refinance later to an amortizing loan! Be sure that it is fixed-rate interest, though. There are lots of interest-only adjustable-rate products around these days. We recommend that you stay away from those! Chairman of the Federal Reserve Board Alan Greenspan warned of "froth" in some markets. Presumably this is one step short of "irrational exuberance." If the market value does drop some time in the future, the people who will get hurt will be the ones who have interest-only loans and have not paid down the principal. They will owe more on the property than it's worth. In the unlikely event that we have a drop in value and a rise in interest rates, those people who have interest-only variable-rate loans may not even be able to make the payments.

I have a credit score of less than 600, and I find it hard to get financing. A mortgage broker that I found on the Internet offered to give me a "credit fixing" loan. It is a high-interest-rate loan but only for two years. Once I've established a good credit rating for two years, they'll refinance at a lower interest rate. Is that a good idea?

There are some low-class mortgage companies around that will give you a great rate for a short time, and then you have to refinance and pay more points. Beware of them. How many points are they going to charge you to refinance in two years? Will they give you a written guarantee that they will refinance the loan then?

It seems almost impossible to make the numbers work in the northern California market. It is so hot—prices keep going up and up. Do you have any advice? I'm still looking for my first buy. What makes sense from a net operating income (NOI) viewpoint?

Remember our philosophy of only buying when the property will support itself. Don't speculate on values going up, and you won't get into trouble. You may need to look in areas further away from the highly desirable neighborhoods. Where do the hotel maids, bus drivers, and store clerks live? These are working-class neighborhoods that you seldom see if you live in affluent areas.

How hard is it to get cash out of a property I just bought and have not fixed up yet? I paid cash for this two-bedroom home with a basement. Now I need to do a little work and would like to pull some cash out.

We're not big advocates of pulling cash out at closing. All that does is cause you to have a bigger mortgage payment. Can you find the money for the fix-up somewhere else and then encumber the property later to get the cash back? You will get a much better deal from a lender if you can wait a year before doing that.

How to Structure the Offer

If I wanted to retire "earlier" through real estate investing, what would I have to do? Buy a lot more property, correct?

Buying correctly is more important that just buying. You can buy a lot of properties that you can't afford to own after you buy them. Focus on buying properties that will at least break even in the beginning, and then let the passage of time and inflation make you rich. Carleton Sheets' Real Estate Toolkit, which is available on our Web site (weekendmillionaire.com) is one of the best real estate tools I know of for people who are serious about investing.

What do you think about the lease-option strategy?

If the seller will lease to you and give you an option at a fixed price, and the rent will cover the outlay, it's a good deal. What doesn't make any sense for an investor is to option at the market-value price to be determined at the time of sale. In such an approach, the seller gets all the benefits of a run-up in market value.

What is the best way to buy single-family residences?

There is no one best way. You have to just keep exploring until you find something that works. Since all properties are different and all people are different, there could be as many different ways to buy property as there are combinations of property and people.

What type of return on investment (ROI) do you look for with your single-family residences?

We don't worry so much about ROI as we do about cash flow. If we can buy a property with the net operating income (NOI) and make it generate cash flow, we feel that we have a good deal. If we're buying with 10 percent down, it would be nice to get a 10 percent return on that down payment, but it's not that significant a factor. ROI becomes more important if you're buying with a large down payment. If you were putting $500,000 down on a large project, you'd want to be sure that you were getting a return on your investment in addition to a cash flow from the property.

I've been rereading your book and am confused about where the return on investment (ROI) on the down payment is added or calculated against the desired bottom line of the net operating income (NOI).

Valuing Single-Family Properties

Return on investment (ROI) is the return you expect on any cash you have to put into the deal. Net operating income (NOI) is what's left after expenses, after the ROI on your cash outlay and before debt service.

Do you have a minimum that you will accept in cash flow, such as $300 a month using your NOI formula?

This depends on the property. No cash flow may be okay for a nice single-family residence in a good area. If a property will break even in the beginning on cash flow, you are still paying down the debt and gaining the appreciation. The longer you own the property, the wider the margin becomes.

I understand the arithmetic of the NOI, but what confuses me is your mention of how the performance of the down payment affected your NOI. For example, if you expected a 5 percent return on what you used for the down payment, how would its performance be considered in the NOI?

If you put $10,000 cash down on a deal and want a 5 percent ROI on that cash, you have to reduce your annual NOI by $500 because you will be paying that to yourself for the use of your money. Then you have to make the loan work with the remaining NOI.

Using your formula for NOI, with a 15-year fixed-rate mortgage, how much cash flow do you need to go ahead? I understand that it is on a case-by-case basis, but what is your lowest cash flow for a great deal?

If we can just break even we're satisfied. When you break even in the beginning, you are still gaining the appreciation and the debt reduction on the mortgage. In time, rents will rise, and cash flow will grow. It depends on the market, but if you could break even with a 15-year loan and pay no more than 20 percent down, it would sound good to us.

How important is ROI in year one?

ROI is increasingly important when you put more cash into the deal. If you can buy for no money down, ROI is a moot point. With a large down payment, we would expect to get a return on that investment in addition to cash flow from the property.

How to Structure the Offer

In your book you talk about making a no-money-down purchase by using bank and seller financing. I don't know if you talked about closing costs in the book. Who pays those?

Closing costs are a negotiable item. Some real estate agents will try to tell you that certain items are your responsibility and others the seller's responsibility. This may be what is generally done, but it's not set in stone, and you may negotiate for the seller to pay all the closing costs, or you may agree to pay them all. Whatever costs you agree to pay, you simply factor those into the purchase offer. They are treated the same as repairs you may need to make to get the property ready to rent. Many times a bank will include the closing costs as part of the financing it provides. With owner financing, closing costs can be negligible.

I have a question for you regarding buying with no money down versus putting your own money down. Using your ROI and NOI formulas, it seems to me that if you can put down 20 percent and gain ROI on it (say, 3 percent) and still get a loan that meets the NOI, it's still a good investment, right? Ideally, putting no money down helps, but as a beginning investor, don't lenders want a 20 percent down payment?

If you're comfortable with 3 percent on your money, and considering that banks are currently only paying 1 to 2 percent, it may be a decent deal. We try to get at least 10 to12 percent on any cash we put into a deal. Don't forget that there are many sources of financing other than conventional lenders. Also remember the benefits of leverage. If you have $40,000 to put down, you control more real estate if you can buy two houses at the same price with $20,000 down on each rather than putting the whole $40,000 into one purchase. Because of leverage, your ultimate ROI will be much higher.

When I read in your book about return on investment (ROI), it was the first time I could see how I could make money on the down payment. Moreover, it really showed me the value of real estate investing beyond the appreciation, tax benefits, etc. What is the best way to maximize this ROI?

The best way is to factor a higher rate of return on your down payment and adjust the NOI accordingly. Then structure deals using the remaining NOI. We use as much seller financing as possible. We've been amazed over the years at the number of sellers who were adamantly opposed to providing financing in our initial discussions but who changed their mind when a contract was presented to them. Banking is like any other business—it's negotiable!

If you can make a 10 to 12 percent ROI on your down payment, are there times when you will put down a larger down payment to get the NOI you need?

No! Because we never put any more of our money into a deal than we absolutely have to. Remember the principle of leverage: The smaller the down payment, the greater is the ROI. If you put $10,000 down on a $100,000 property and the property appreciates 5 percent per year, the appreciation alone gives you a 50 percent return on your cash. On the other hand, if you put $50,000 down on a $100,000 property and it appreciates 5 percent per year, the appreciation only represents a 10 percent return on your cash. Also, you're conserving your capital for future investment opportunities or to hold as cash reserves. With cash in the bank, we have options that we don't have if it's tied up in real estate equity. Once you have a property or two paid for, often you can borrow against one and get the money to pay cash for a new purchase, and doing this is the same as making a no-money-down deal. And that's the time that you can really accelerate ROI!

Can you pool the equity in several properties to get a revolving line of credit similar to an equity line on your personal home?

It can be done, but be very careful of blanket encumbrances because they restrict your options so much. You might want to sell one of those properties, and all of them are tied up unless you can get the lender to release one of them, and to do that, you'd have to have plenty of equity in the other properties. Never blanket-encumber properties unless you have release clauses built into the note. The amount is negotiable, but lenders typically require a 25 percent bonus on the amount of the release. Let's say that you have a million-dollar loan and the property you want released represents 10 percent of the value of the properties that secure the loan. You may be expected to pay the loan down by $125,000, which is 10 percent plus the 25 percent release bonus. This gives the lender additional security in the remaining properties covered by the blanket loan. Don't offer a blanket encumbrance unless you really know what you're doing. If fact, we listed it in the last chapter of *The Weekend Millionaire's Secrets to Investing in Real Estate* as one of the 14 biggest mistakes that beginning investors make. We suggest that you read it and the other thirteen as well.

How do you get a 30-year fixed-rate loan on investment property? The last apartment building I bought I could only get a fixed rate for 5 years.

Shop around more. You may be able to get a standard mortgage for investor owners with a 30-year fixed rate and possibly even have the first 10-year period be interest-only. There are many financing products available in the market today, so you don't have to accept the first offer.

When you use interest-only loans, are you paying your mortgage down as well?

No, you are not paying your mortgage down. Therefore, only do it for a short period of time until you can refinance the property and start building equity. We don't like interest-only loans, but for a new investor, they can be a way to build equity through appreciation while you are getting started. We like to get properties paid off as quickly as possible. The cash flow is great when you don't have any debt. Avoid interest-only loans that have a variable interest rate.

Why is most of the financing you talk about in the book a 15-year loan?

Because that's what we used when we were getting started. It's a good compromise between low payments and starting to pay down the loan much faster than with a 30-year loan. We had very little cash flow for years, but we're doing quite well now. About 70 percent of what we own is owned free and clear.

I understand that 30-year loans give extra cash flow and you're using the bank's money as long as possible. What about 40-year loans?

A 40-year loan is just about an interest-only loan. We would never do that. The payments on a 40-year loan are not that much lower than on a 30-year loan. Let's assume a $200,000 loan at 7 percent interest rate. Payments on a

40-year loan would be $1,243 per month. Payments on a 30-year loan would be $1,330 per month, which is $87 a month more. However, over the life of the loan, you would pay $117,558 less in interest. This sounds like a good deal to us. And if you recover your capital faster, you will buy more properties sooner, giving you more growth through appreciation on more properties.

My first two properties have interest-only loans. I'm just wondering when to cross over from interest-only to 15-year fixed-rate loans, as discussed in your book? At some point in time I want to have investments with no debt.

This is a question only you can answer. The interest-only loans give you more cash flow now but less down the road than you would have if you paid off the loans. The sooner you get started paying off the loans, and the less time you take to do so, the sooner you can start enjoying the real cash flow that comes from properties owned free and clear.

Your return on equity is low on paid-off properties, so you could sell one old house and buy four or five new houses using 80 percent financing and get much more cash flow and much more appreciation, couldn't you?

You are correct, but just as in the board game Monopoly, there comes a point when your cash flow is great enough to keep buying for cash. You also can refinance paid-for properties and use the money to purchase additional ones, which accomplishes much the same thing as you would if you sold the properties to get the cash, and you don't have to pay tax like you do on a sale.

What's your philosophy on using leverage to buy things other than real estate, such as cars, planes, and boats?

Our philosophy on airplanes and other big toys is that if you have to borrow money to buy them, you aren't ready to own them. Leverage is a very simple concept. If it's going to go up in value, use as little cash as you can; if it's going to go down in value, pay cash.

How would you foreclose on a tax-lien if you purchased one?

You can buy tax liens from the county or state. They usually have sales once a year. Then you need to start the foreclosure process. You would have to have the property sold on the courthouse steps, and then you would bid in the amount of the lien, just as a lender would do. Then, if you get outbid, you get your money for the lien. If you are not outbid, you will get a judgment deed for the property.

When you look at a house and you figure what it will take to fix it up, how do you find out what it will appraise for?

We don't care what the house appraises for. Appraisals are for banks, not investors. If you buy according to the way we teach, you will have no problem with appraisals.

I've heard that a higher appraisal helps you to pay less out of pocket at closing. Would I be able to get no-money-down loans if the purchase price is 90 percent of the appraised value or better?

This is only true after you've been at it a long time and built a track record with your lenders. In the meantime, most lenders will want 80 percent of appraisal or 80 percent of cost, whichever is less. If you can purchase at 70 percent or less of the appraised value, you may be able to get 100 percent financing.

I didn't find in your books how to account for a declining house price market. That's a real danger, isn't it?

Rental prices tend to be stable even when selling prices go down. Remember that we advocate buying and holding. As long as the property is generating enough rent to cover the cost of owning it, it doesn't matter if the value of the property drops for a while. We've seen sales prices rise and fall dramatically with very little effect on rents. We think that this still holds true. In the early 1990s in California, we saw selling prices drop by 25 percent, but that didn't create bargains for renters. There is a market for rents and a market for sales, and they have little to do with one another. Proof is that a 1,600-square-foot house will lease for about the same in almost any major metropolitan area, but they cost much more to buy in San Francisco than in Fort Worth. The stable rent and fluctuating price situation is what makes it sometimes easy to find deals and sometimes hard.

Another piece of info I have heard on the news lately here is that 25 percent of all homes now sold in Phoenix are sold to investors. Is this out of line or what?

Valuing Single-Family Properties

This is possible. We've heard the same thing about the Miami condo market. A recent *Newsweek* article showed Redding, CA, Medford, OR, Pocatello, ID, Visalia, CA, and Punta Gorda, FL, as towns where over 20 percent of purchasers are investors. If you're in an area like that, we recommend that you approach deals with more caution. Too many investor-owned properties in an area can cause big fluctuations in prices. One of our readers told us about a local neighborhood where he wouldn't buy because an investor group bought up entire blocks of houses. Streets with "For Lease" signs on every house are not good places to be investing.

High prices and low rents are making it nearly impossible to buy houses for the right price to rent out and get cash flow. I'm looking only at properties I think would rent well. The only concern I have with any deal is that if I make a mistake or the NOI drops or I can't rent it, I might have a loan with a balance greater than I can sell it for to get out of the deal. Shouldn't I be concerned about that?

The key to success is to make offers that work for you and keep on making them until one is accepted. Real estate investing is not risk-free, but it's 10 times safer than the stock market and 3 times safer than putting your money under the mattress, where it could get stolen! If you buy using the NOI as a guide, you won't have that problem. You will be buying at 60 to 80 percent of appraised value.

I have a couple of single-family homes already but have been looking at a duplex today. I know that you suggest sticking with single-family homes early on. Why? And what are the main differences I should be looking at?

There isn't much difference in strategy between a duplex and a single-family home. However, there are expenses associated with multifamily properties that aren't there with single-family homes. These would include common-area maintenance, utilities, grounds maintenance, etc.

How do rehab costs figure into NOI and ROI calculations?

We'd figure it just the way we tell you in the book. Determine the cost of the rehab work, decide how much return you want on the money you will put into the work, and then factor that into calculating how much you want to pay for the property in its existing state.

The homes I looked at need a significant amount of rehab. I was estimating the cost and then subtracting the monthly payment amount to cover these rehabs from the NOI; the rest was used to calculate the amount that can go toward the mortgage. Does this sound correct?

Yes, that's right. It's easier to understand if you think of borrowing the money for the rehab rather than using your own money. Then you need to have enough NOI to make the payments on the rehab loan and still have enough rental income left over to make the mortgage payment. If you plan to use your own cash for the rehab work, you need to have enough NOI to pay yourself the return you are looking to get and enough left over to make the mortgage payment.

I have some units under contract, and on due diligence, I found the roof to be around 18 years old and some units in need of paint and carpeting. Should I ask for a lower price or some money back at closing to cover part of cost? Or can I do that at all?

We would determine what the value would be based on the properties being fixed up and in good condition and then would make our offers minus the amount it would take to put them in that condition. We'd certainly test the water by asking for concessions. How well you do will depend on how many options the seller has. If you can get the seller to do the repairs or give you a cash-at-closing allowance to make the repairs, you're that much better off. We would make the argument that some items needing to be done could be considered normal wear and tear. But other items, such as an 18-year-old roof, could be considered deferred maintenance that the owner should have taken care of.

What ROI percentage are you using on money invested? I've been using 10 percent.

The best answer is "all you can get." However, a good rule of thumb would be at least prime rate plus 3 percent. This is about what it would cost a new investor to borrow money from a bank.

Valuing Single-Family Properties

I know that you base your purchase price on the NOI and whether it will cover expenses and debt service. Do you also have a capitalization rate that you look at as well or a certain profit margin above and beyond the debt service (such as $100 per house or $50 per unit)?

If we can buy a property that will just break even in the beginning after considering all expenses and vacancy, we consider it a good deal because the longer you own the property, the higher the margins will get as rents increase and debt pays down.

I live in Chicago, where average single-family home prices are relatively high. It seems that to achieve success using your model and using leverage, I need to focus on homes that are in the range of $150,000 and below in order to be successful. Am I misunderstanding this? I don't see how one can purchase a home for $250,000 and above with 20 percent or less down and still break even on cash flow, even if $250,000 or $300,000 is 50 percent below market. Isn't that so?

The numbers in the book are for illustrative purposes only. The price range varies from market to market. "Bread and butter" properties may list for $75,000 to $90,000 in one market, $100,000 to $120,000 in another, and $150,000 to $200,000 in another. This range is also reflected by the rents these properties will command in a given market. A house may sell for $80,000 and rent for $600 to $800 per month in one market, and the exact same house may cost $175,000 and rent for $1,300 to $1,600 per month in another market. What's important is that you find deals that you can purchase with the NOI.

I saw nothing in your NOI calculations for things such as snow removal, waste removal, landscaping, utilities, etc. Is it common that renters of single-family homes pay these costs and bear these burdens themselves? What about closing costs, title searches, etc.?

The items you mention are usually covered by the renter in single-family homes; however, if you will be responsible for them, by all means add them to the expense items when calculating NOI. Closing costs and title searches typically are split in some way between the buyer and the seller. An agent will

tell you what is customary in your area; however, closing costs can be negotiated with the seller.

*I met someone who has over 200 rental houses, and they are all Section 8.
He has been doing this for about 20 years. He also buys "as is" houses and
sells them wholesale. He told me that he would help me get started if I buy
properties from him. He will show me how to buy them wholesale, fix them
up, and refinance them, and I should be able to put some cash in my pocket
after each deal. He told me to Section 8 the properties because that will
ensure that I get my rent every month. The average house wholesale is
about $40,000. They retail for about $65,000. His goal is to have $100 a
month positive cash flow from each property. After 15 years, the property
is paid off. I figure his properties are worth about $10 million and that he
is generating about $125,000 a month from rent. I don't know if this is a
good way to get started in real estate. He is very successful at this way of
doing it. He said that this is how he got started. The properties he has are
about 20 to 30 miles from my house. Most of the houses need a lot of work.
He told me that he knows people to help fix them up. He told me he wants
me to be successful at it so that I will keep buying his houses. I am not sure
if I should follow in this person's way of doing this. He is very nice and
seems like he wants to help me. The way I figure, he is doing well enough
without me buying his properties. Should I work with him, or do you think
this is not a good way to get started?*

We would recommend that you apply the criteria we outline in the book to
the deals this gentleman wants to sell you. If the numbers work, the properties could be good deals. One question that comes to our minds is, "If this
man is doing so well, why does he want to sell his properties?" When you
sell, you cap your profits at the time of sale. When you hold properties, they
can continue to earn income for the rest of your life.

[Section 8 is a federal rent-subsidy program. The U.S. Department of
Housing and Urban Development (HUD) will inspect your property each
year and confirm that the rent you're charging is in line. Currently, a family of four can get a subsidy if their total income is less that $26,500. You still
have to find and approve the tenants. You get a government check for the
subsidy at the start of the month.]

As for Section 8, we don't know a lot about it because we don't have any properties in the program. The few Mike has had in the past were not good experiences, which is why he doesn't have any Section 8 tenants now. Maybe he just had bad luck, but every Section 8 tenant he had left the property needing significant repairs before it could be rerented. Roger's experience was better. The plus side to Section 8 is that you don't have to worry where the tenant is going to get the rent money.

On your NOI form you do not factor in a mortgage payment. Is the theory that your mortgage payment should be at or below your NOI to make the deal work? I can input the numbers and get a $700 monthly NOI and 14 percent ROI (including ROI on down payment). However, my mortgage payment (P&I) would be $750 per month. To me this looks like a negative cash flow but positive ROI. Could you please clarify where the mortgage payment should be included in the formulas?

NOI is the money left over after covering all your expenses. The reason it doesn't include the mortgage payment is because it's the money from which you will make that payment. In your example, you have a $700 NOI but are looking at a $750 payment. This tells me that you need to change your offer to get the payment to $700 or less. There are several ways to do this: You can offer less, lengthen the loan repayment period, ask for a lower interest rate on the loan, or some combination of the three. A payment of $700 will cover a $78,000 loan at 7 percent for 15 years, a $90,000 loan at 7 percent for 20 years, an $88,500 loan at 5 percent for 15 years, or a $126,000 loan at 0 percent for 15 years. These are just a few of the hundreds of variables that can get the payment down to the NOI or less.

In your book you mention that we should get loans for 15 to 20 years. I've calculated my NOI ($7,644 per year) and divided it by the percentage of the loan at 30 years (5.21 percent), which gives me a purchase price of $138,453. When I run the numbers with 15- or 20-year loans, the numbers don't work. What's the problem with me getting a 30-year loan to make this work for me?

The reason we mentioned 15- to 20-year financing in the book is because that's what most of the banks like to do with investor loans. You should use whatever length of loan you feel comfortable using. There is no hard and fast rule in this regard. Your age should be considered, because if you are 25, you may feel differently about a 30-year loan than someone who is 65.

In The Weekend Millionaire's Secrets to Investing in Real Estate *you recommend 15-year mortgages. Our cash flow on a 15-year mortgage (5.5 percent) would be $100 per month. If we were to put it on 30 years (6 percent), our cash flow would be $300 per month. I posted this same question on a message board and was told to go with 30-year mortgages. Our debt-to-income ratio is under 20 percent, and our goal is to buy one house per year for rental purposes for the next 10 years. Would you recommend a 15-year or a 30-year mortgage?*

Whether you use 15- or 30-year financing is entirely up to you. Yes, 30-year financing will give you a larger cash flow now, but the payments will continue for 15 more years after the property would be paid off with a 15-year mortgage. If you have something you need the additional cash flow for now and can reinvest it for a greater return than allowing it to pay off the mortgage early, by all means do so. We have always used 15-year financing, which is why today we enjoy being in a position where about 70 percent of all our properties are owned free and clear. This really improves your cash flow. Your goal of buying one property a year is realistic and very doable. You should have no problem meeting it. As you gain more experience, you probably will increase the goal to two, three, or more properties per year.

I am presently reading The Weekend Millionaire's Secrets to Investing in Real Estate, *and I am running into a hurdle that I don't know how to overcome. In Dallas, Texas, and surrounding areas the property taxes are very high, in the 2.3 to 3.2 percent range. This is causing me to have a very low NOI. For example, a house that retails for $100,000 will rent for around $900 to $1,000 per month. Using the factors that you used in the chapter "Valuing Single-Family Properties," which I think is low on the insurance amount, I get an NOI of $468 at a $100,000 purchase price and $537 at a $70,000 purchase price. The corresponding payments are much higher than the NOI, even for 30-year terms. It seems to me that I will have to get* *a seller not only to give a large discount but also to carry a very large second at a very low interest rate to even get close to making this work. Where am I missing it?*

We're glad to hear that you are reading our book. We hope that by the time you finish, it will answer most of your questions. We're not sure how you are doing your calculations because when you say you "get an NOI of $468 at a $100,000 purchase price and $537 at a $70,000 purchase price," we don't follow you. Purchase price should have no bearing on NOI calculations. NOI is used to calculate value not price. A $1,000 per month NOI could support a $100,000 loan financed at just under 9 percent for 15 years or a $180,000 loan at 0 percent for the same 15 years. At either price, $1,000 per month for 15 years would cover the loan. Granted, these are two extremes, but between them are a wide range of combinations of price and terms that may work for many sellers, and all being within the NOI. You should first calculate the NOI and then use it to develop various combinations of price and terms to try to come up with something that will work for each seller. Yes, you do need to find sellers willing to discount the price or the terms to make deals work. This is buying at wholesale, and it's what you have to do to be a successful investor. Think about this! Most people work 40 hours a week, 50 weeks a year, for 40 years and end up with little more to show for it than a meager retirement with Social Security. If it takes you an entire year of making offers to buy your first property and buy it right, within 15 or so years, that one property probably will pay you more than Social Security for which you worked your whole life. Imagine if by spending just four hours a week you could buy one property a year for 15 years.

I just read the Weekend Millionaire *book. Good stuff. I'm just stuck on one point: Page 153 implies that the length of a note doesn't affect its value. This implies that the following notes, all based on a sale price of $80,000, have monthly payments of $680:*

15 years at 6.113 percent

20 years at 8.217 percent

25 years at 9.157 percent

How to Structure the Offer

Sure, if you plug them in to a financial calculator and compute the present value of each, they all come out to the same $80,000 sale price. But as a buyer, I would always prefer the first choice. It is clearly more valuable to me than the other two. But I can't figure out the math to use to demonstrate that.

We agree with you! Your first choice is also our first choice! We believe that a wholesale purchase of real estate should be one that will allow the cash flow to pay for the property in 15 years. Some people disagree with us, but that's been our formula for over 25 years. The examples we gave in the book all work and are all basically the same unless, like us, you want to pay for your properties in 15 years. Set your own criteria, and then live by it.

What we're talking about here is the time value of money. In the example, you have two constants, $680 per month NOI and a price of $80,000. The example was used to illustrate how when the price is fixed and the NOI is known; if you raise the interest rate on your offer, you have to adjust the length of the loan in order to stay within your payment amount. In this example, if you are going to use $80,000 of someone else's money (the loan), the amount you are going to pay them to use it (the interest rate) determines how long it will take you to pay it back when the payment is fixed ($680 per month). The more of the payment that goes to cover interest, the less there is to reduce principal, which means that it takes longer to pay back the borrowed money. If you didn't have to pay any interest, the $680 payment would pay back the loan in less than 10 years.

We know this all sounds confusing, but the reason the deals used in the example are the same is because in each case you are using $80,000 of someone else's money and paying for the use of it until it is all paid back. When calculating the time value of money, there are four factors: price, interest rate, length of loan, and payment amount. If you know any three of these, you can compute the fourth.

Since we don't want you to put yourself into a negative-cash-flow situation, we teach you to calculate the NOI and let it be your "payment constant" (monthly amount available to buy the property). This means that of the remaining three items that enter the equation (price, interest rate, and length of loan), one must be adjusted if the other two are fixed (e.g., price and interest rate fixed, length of loan must be adjusted; price and length of loan fixed, interest rate must be adjusted; interest rate and length of loan fixed, price must be adjusted).

We use 15 years as a fixed length of loan, which means that we adjust the price and the interest rate in order to buy properties with the NOI and pay for them in 15 years. Don't forget that while you are paying off the loan with a fixed payment, the rents probably are going to rise with inflation, so you won't necessarily have 15 years of no cash flow.

You don't mention private mortgage insurance (PMI) in the book. Banks here require PMI for anything less than 20 percent down (or 80 percent financing). Is it the same in other parts of the country? How do you handle this additional expense? Is your basic presumption that you'll be buying the house for at least 20 percent below market value? I think the banks only look at the purchase price and not the market or appraised value when determining PMI.

Private mortgage insurance is pretty much standard with conventional bank financing when you borrow more than 80 percent of the purchase price, but banks are just one of many sources of financing. Private mortgages and "owner will carry" mortgages make up a large percentage of investor financing. Keep in mind that to be successful investing in rental properties, you must buy them wholesale. This means that the price, the terms, or a combination of the two must produce a wholesale value. If you only consider conventional bank financing, you will severely limit your possibilities.

I understand owner-will-carry (OWC) financing, but can you expand on private mortgages?

As we use the term here, "private mortgages" include OWC mortgages as well as any other mortgages provided by private investors. There are many people who choose to invest in mortgages rather than real estate, stocks, bonds, CDs, etc. These investors provide financing for many real estate purchases and often can be located through mortgage brokers.

25

Structuring
Your First Deal

For all new investors, structuring your first deal is a traumatic experience. Questions run through your mind like: "What if I miscalculate
the numbers?" "What if I can't get the financing?" "What if I make the sellers mad with my offer?" "What if I can't make the payments?" And dozens
more! We had these concerns when we first started, and you will too.

All investments have risks, and real estate is no different. The art is to
minimize the risk by learning as much as possible about the property, the
neighborhood, market conditions, rental demand, and other such factors
that can affect the profitability of a transaction. If you err, be sure to err on
the side of caution, and it will serve you well. No one ever got hurt by a property they didn't buy.

When structuring your first deal, be sure the offers you make will work
for you under your current conditions. This may mean that you make many
offers before you have one accepted, but we feel that it is critically important
for new investors to have their first transaction be a good one. In this chapter of *The Weekend Millionaire's Secrets to Investing in Real Estate*, we

took readers through a hypothetical analysis of a property and gave them several ways to make offers that the calculated net operating income (NOI) would support.

We have received thousands of questions on this topic and have tried to consolidate the ones that were similar into the following.

Is there such a thing as a property that is too much of a bargain?

Some of the best buys we've made seemed overpriced at the time. Some of the worst buys we've made looked like sensational bargains when we bought them. There are three elements to a real estate market: buyers who want to buy, sellers who want to sell, and ample available financing. When all three of these elements are in place, a property that is priced fairly and given adequate marketing should sell quickly. If a property has been on the market long enough for the seller to take a low offer, it was either overpriced to begin with, or there are some inherent problems that may not be apparent that stopped buyers from making offers. Perhaps the neighborhood has an unsavory reputation, and you don't know the area well enough to realize that it's a problem. These hidden negative factors will make other buyers shy away from the property should you ever want to sell. This is why we say that you should do your homework; research an area before you buy, especially if a deal looks too good to be true.

Since the Weekend Millionaire program is a buy-and-hold strategy and you never intend to sell the property, why does it matter if you buy in a less than desirable neighborhood? After all, you aren't intending to sell the property anytime soon.

In the long run, the lack of desirability decreases your equity value and your borrowing power against that property. Even if you never sell the property, you still want it to go up in value. The Weekend Millionaire program says that you don't intend to sell the property, but you want it to go up in value so that you can increase rents and eventually borrow against the equity to buy more properties. A more desirable area enhances both these goals.

After reading your books and listening to your CDs, I have changed the way I look at financing properties. I've always thought that if I keep refinanc-

ing every five years and pulling money out without having to pay taxes on it, I would be better off. Now I'm wondering if paying off the loans and building cash flow is the best way to go. Do you believe that it's more important to pay off the loans and develop cash flow than to keep refinancing?

Underlying our entire philosophy is the belief that wealth is an income stream. You can go broke owning things unless they are generating cash flow for you. Owning a lot of property may give you bragging rights at an investment club, but we'd rather brag about the cash flow that the properties are generating. True financial independence only comes when your unearned income is adequate to support your lifestyle. It's not what you own; its how much cash it is generating that's most important.

Do you think that it is better to borrow money from the seller or from commercial lenders?

We don't think it matters much who finances a purchase. Go with what makes the numbers work. The advantage you get with owner financing is flexibility. An owner can decide to accept any interest rate he or she wants or to charge no interest if he or she wants. It's a great opportunity to create a win for both the seller and the buyer. Every seller has different needs. A seller who is retiring may not want cash as much as he or she needs an income stream. A seller who is retiring five years from now may not want any cash for the next five years but wants to create an income stream at the time. Being able to fulfill the needs of the seller is the big advantage of dealing with owner financing. It's essential that you see it from the seller's point of view, not yours. What you would do if you were the seller has nothing to do with it.

Have you heard of the 65 percent rule for determining the maximum allowable offer (MAO)? I didn't see any of that in your approaches.

This is the calculation used by some real estate gurus. It says that you should estimate the value of the property after repairs have been made and not pay more that 65 percent of that value minus the cost of repairs. This seems like a safe bet, but getting sellers to accept an offer that low is something else! We feel more confident having a property manager recommend to us what a property will rent for and then calculate the value based on that rental amount. The missing factor from this formula is the financing. If you can get the seller to carry back financing at a low or 0 percent interest rate, you may be able to pay full asking price for a property and still have the present value of the deal be 65 percent or less of the price you pay.

If I have $100,000 cash to work with, are there any particular techniques I should stick to?

Use your $100,000 wisely. Make offers that use the smallest amounts of cash necessary to put the deals together. Even when you have a lot of cash, you maximize your return when you use the magic of leverage. Your return will be far greater if you can buy five $100,000 houses and put $20,000 down on each than if you buy one house for that price and pay all cash. Of course, you want to be sure that the net operating income (NOI) will support the mortgages on the five houses. The biggest advantage is that you are gaining appreciation on $500,000 rather than $100,000 worth of property and having inflation increases in the rent on five rentals rather than one.

What is my best bet for financing on my first property?

We'd recommend asking for seller financing in the beginning. Sellers can be much more flexible in the terms they offer, and closing costs are minimal. You may not get it, but it doesn't hurt to ask, and you always can turn to conventional financing if the deal is good enough.

With the availability of cheap money and a sellers' market, do sellers still give terms on their property?

Absolutely! It may be hard for you to believe, but not all sellers need or want cash, especially while interest rates are so low. We had someone recently turn down our initial offer for cash and two months later come back to us with an offer to take back financing if we were still interested in the property. We had assumed that they needed cash, but after the person's CPA told him about the tax advantages of not taking all the equity out at once, the seller decided that financing the purchase for a solid buyer wasn't all that bad. Another good negotiating strategy is to point out to sellers what the banks will pay them for their money if they deposit it. You can then offer to pay them more than the bank will pay but less than the bank will charge for a loan. People don't advertise seller financing, and most probably haven't even thought about it. This is why we suggest making two offers, one for cash and one asking for financing. See which one the seller is most attracted to. By making two offers and using the seller's response to guide us on which way to go, we very often smoke out people willing to finance. In the old days of assumable loans, sellers carrying back a second was very common. Now, with the advent of the "due-on-sale" clause, we need to find sellers with a lot of equity to make it work.

Can you start successfully with price and then switch to terms?

Rather than start with one and then try to switch, we recommend making two offers in the beginning, one for cash and the other with the seller carrying back financing. This not only projects strength as a buyer, but it also gives the seller a wide range of prices to consider. Here's an example: A property with a $1,000 per month NOI would support a $100,000 mortgage payable over 15 years at about 9 percent or a $180,000 mortgage payable over the same period at 0 percent. This gives a price range of $80,000, and somewhere between those extremes there may be a combination of price and terms that will work for the seller. Base your offers on NOI, but structure them to meet the seller's needs.

When making an offer that asks the seller to carry back financing, should you try to meet the asking price?

Offers that meet the asking price always get more consideration that ones that seem "low ball" unless the seller is desperate to unload the property. By asking for favorable terms, you often can offer more than the asking price and still get a better deal than you could get with a substantial discount for cash.

Is it legally possible to still do "subject to" existing financing purchases?

Yes, if you inform the lender and disclose the transaction to the lender. Otherwise, you are deceiving the lender by allowing the lender to think that the original owner is still in the property. There are people who will tell you that you can have the seller put the property into a trust and then buy an interest in the trust without the lender finding out that the property has been sold. You're still deceiving the lender, and we would never recommend that anyone do that. Some states are considering legislation to require not only that the lenders be notified but also that the sellers and buyers be informed of the potential liability they face in such transactions.

What do you think of using a negative-amortizing loan to make a deal work? Lots of mortgage brokers in California are offering negative-amortizing adjustable-rate mortgages (neg. ARMS). Are they a good idea?

("Negative amortizing" means that you are paying less than the interest due each month, and the amount of principal owed is growing.) Using negative-amortizing loans may make your cash flow work, but each year you owe more and more on the property. Stay away from them. As time goes by, your cash flow should increase as you raise rents, and the amount you owe should decrease as you pay the loan down. We'd strongly advise staying away from any negative-amortizing loans. And an adjustable-interest-rate negative-amortizing loan is like playing Russian roulette—don't do it!

Now that you have so many properties and a hefty monthly cash flow, do you buy your properties for cash, or do you still finance them with a bank?

We still finance all new purchases. To pay cash is to lose one of the great advantages of real estate investing—being able to leverage a lot of real estate with a relatively small amount of cash invested. We don't want to buy the properties with our money; we want the tenants to buy them for us.

How do you buy your properties nowadays? Do you use a home-equity line of credit (HELOC), pay cash, or take out a mortgage?

Yes, all the above!

Does a HELOC affect your FICO score when you first take it out because it can be maxed out initially?

Your FICO score is affected by the amount of the loan whether you draw on it or not. This is so because the money is instantly available to you. Incidentally, FICO stands for Fair, Isaac Corporation, a company started by Bill Fair and Earl Isaac, who were consultants in San Francisco during the 1950s when credit cards were first becoming popular. They were early leaders in developing credit scores for their customers, who were retailers, finance houses, and mail-order firms. Now you know.

This week my attorney mentioned a 24-unit deal that he is working on but can't finance alone. It cash flows heavily, but I am skeptical about going into a partnership with someone else. Do you think this would be a good way for me to get started?

You need to make that call yourself. If you feel comfortable with partners, go ahead, but do so with the awareness that partnerships can be as volatile a business relationship as you can get into. The reason we don't have partners is because we don't need them, and we prefer to have control. If you go into a partnership, be sure that you have an agreement that considers every possible development, and have another attorney write it with the assumption that, by the time you need it, you and your partner will be screaming at each other.

Would you pay more than the appraised value of a property if you could get the right terms, such as a lot of owner financing?

Yes, we've done that several times, especially when we have been able to obtain 0 percent financing from the seller. What's important is that the NOI will cover the payments.

What if it isn't 0 percent financing, just a regular note . . . but it still kicks off a great cash flow?

As long as the cash flow works, you should be fine. Just remember that covering all the expenses and the debt service is what's really important to a buy-and-hold investor. You don't want to own properties that deplete your cash flow.

In your book you talk a lot about 15-year financing. Would you consider a property to be a good buy if the NOI only will cover the debt service on 30-year financing, or would you expect a certain amount of cash flow right away before a 30-year loan would make sense?

This depends on the circumstances. Thirty-year financing is fine for buyers who are young and have many years ahead of them before retirement, but if you look carefully at it, when interest rates are low, the difference in payments between a 15-year loan and 30-year loan is not all that great.

What do you think of starting out with 30-year financing and then accelerating payments as the rents go up so that you can pay it off in less that 30 years. Does this sound like a good idea?

It sounds like a good plan if you will stick to it. With most people, the problem is they start with good intentions, but the temptation to spend the excess cash instead of paying it on the loan often gets the best of them.

What about loans that contain a prepayment penalty clause? Since you don't plan to sell the property anyway, does it really matter if the loan has this clause?

We never sign a note with a prepayment penalty. A "due-on-sale" clause is standard these days, but prepayment clauses are no longer acceptable. Some lenders try to include them on loans that have a low initial rate that goes up after, say, three years. This discourages you from taking advantage of the low rate and then refinancing. Usually a prepayment penalty does not apply after the loan has matured for a number of years. Another reason for a prepayment penalty is if the borrower has marginal credit. The lender wants to give itself an extra margin because of the higher likelihood of the borrower defaulting.

If the only way to get a positive cash flow is through an interest-only loan, is that okay in your opinion?

We don't like interest-only loans unless they are just for a year or two before the amortization starts. The only interest-only loans we use are lines of credit.

I'm trying to buy my first property, and I'm planning to offer the seller 60 percent cash, which I will get from a first-mortgage loan, and then ask the seller to carry back 40 percent on a second mortgage. Do you think that this will work?

Not knowing the seller's situation, it's hard to tell. If the seller has enough equity in the property, you would find it easier to get a 40 percent first mortgage with the owner carrying back 60 percent of the financing. If it's a good property, you should be able to get a 40 percent loan if you can fog a mirror because the first-mortgage lender knows the seller is not going to let it foreclose on the loan and wipe out his second.

Why do you feel that it is easier getting 40 percent financing than 60 percent? I haven't done a lot of non-owner-occupied (NOO) loans, but I have never had a problem getting people qualified for 60 percent loan-to-value (LTV) ratio loans. Does a lower LTV ratio really make that much of a difference?

See the answer to the preceding question. The more a seller finances on a second mortgage, the less risk there is for a default on the first. Think about it: If you sold a property for $100,000, the buyer got a first mortgage for $40,000 and gave that cash to you, and you financed the rest, would you ever allow the holder of the first mortgage to foreclose and wipe out your $60,000 mortgage?

When you're getting started, what do you do about insurance? Do you have to get a separate policy for each property?

On your first deal and probably the next few after it, you will need to get a separate policy for each property. Once you acquire several properties, you can get a large blanket policy that covers everything. You should discuss this with your insurance agent because each company has different underwriting requirements that must be met before it will issue a blanket policy.

Should a first offer ask for financing if you don't know what position the sellers are in?

There's no reason it shouldn't. You may never find out if an owner will finance if you don't ask. We say don't be afraid to ask for anything; all the seller can do is say no.

26

How to Write the Offer

Of all the things you will do as you start your real estate investing career, writing your first offer will produce your most anxious moments. As with anything else unfamiliar, the more offers you make, the easier it will get. One way to overcome the anxiety of writing offers is to think of them as nothing more than writing down what you are willing to do to purchase someone's property. These written offers can take any form from formal fill-in-the-blanks offer forms to something as simple as handwritten notes on the back of a grocery bag.

An offer is just that, an offer, until it is accepted by the seller, and consideration is paid. When a seller accepts your offer to purchase, you will want to transfer it to a more formal agreement that can be signed by both parties and pay a deposit into escrow as a sign of good faith and to insure your performance. One reason for using more formalized offer-to-purchase agreements is because there are so many things that need to be addressed when buying real estate; it's easier to create a form that addresses most of them and one that simply can be signed by the sellers if they agree with the offer.

How to Structure the Offer

In this chapter of *The Weekend Millionaire's Secrets to Investing in Real Estate,* we tried to take our readers through each item that a contract should include and explain what each means and why it is important. Although we addressed each item individually, we didn't cover the questions dealing with uncertainty and anxiety that all new investors experience. Here are some of those questions.

I have a question about a house on which we made an offer. The seller came back with a counteroffer "as is." We found out that the septic system was partially covered over with a concrete slab and is essentially inaccessible to servicing. Can we back out of the offer because the septic does not comply with code? We put down earnest money, and we don't want to lose it.

Unless you accepted the counteroffer with the "as is" stipulation, you do not have a contract and should have no problem getting your earnest money back. When an offer is accepted by the sellers, but changes are made to your original offer, it does not become a contract until you accept the changes. If you did accept the counteroffer, your deposit money is at risk, but it doesn't mean you're out of options. If the problem with the septic tank was not disclosed to you, you may have a way out of the contract. Also, is the concrete slab that big a problem? Septic tanks only need to be serviced every several years. The expense to break out the concrete to pump the tank may not be enough to lose the deal over.

When you talk about making offers, are you making a verbal offer, or is it in a letter of intent? What is the vehicle you use to make the offer to a seller?

We use a lot of letters of intent advising that if our offer is acceptable, it will be expanded immediately to contract form. If possible, we like to meet with the sellers before sending a letter of intent. In this way we can find out more about their circumstances and structure a better offer.

If interest rates go up, will it be harder to get sellers to carry back financing?

It could work both ways. When interest rates go up, sellers can get higher returns on their investment portfolios, so creative financing is less attractive to them. However, if interest rates go up, property will be harder to sell, and sellers may be more willing to be creative in the terms they offer.

How to Write the Offer

How hard is it to find properties?

We have so many people tell us that they can't find properties when what they are actually saying is that they are afraid to make offers that work for them and would prefer to listen to the bankers and real estate agents tell them what they should do. Listening to real estate agents and bankers telling you that your investment plan won't work is a sure-fire way to get discouraged. As one of our students put it, "If you haven't had your real estate agent tell you you're crazy yet, you're not trying hard enough."

When you get owner financing, do you get the sellers to agree to "substitution of collateral"?

We always put that in our offers. Sometimes we get it, and sometimes we don't. We've only had to use it once in our careers. A "substitution of collateral" clause gives you the right to substitute another piece of property of equal or greater value to secure the sellers' carry-back loan. Some sellers will agree to this and some won't, but asking for it gives you a good negotiating tool. You may be able to get a much more important concession from the sellers in exchange for dropping the substitution-of-collateral clause.

Do you always get a title search prior to purchasing? And if so, do you put it in the offer that it is subject to a clean title search? Also, do you use a title company, or are there any good online companies?

Always get a title search done by a real estate attorney or a title company, and insist on being able to obtain title insurance. Your offer should be made subject to your approval of the title report, which is better than "subject to a clean title search." That might be open to interpretation. Many title companies will do free preliminary title searches as a way to attract your business. We don't know of any way you can search titles online, but more and more counties are starting to make their public records available over the Internet.

What's the difference between a preliminary title search and a full title search? Do you ever get a full search?

The full search comes when you buy title insurance. Since everything is computerized these days, there's not much difference between the two. In

161

the old days, a title officer would search the records manually, just skimming them for the preliminary report (called a "prelim") and doing a more thorough search before he or she would issue the full policy. Some states use attorneys for title searches, and in some states you go directly to the title company. Always get a full title search before buying. Of course, commercial lenders demand that you do it and obtain a lender's title policy to protect them when they make your loan.

Who pays for title insurance?

Each state has customary ways of doing things, and these can even vary from one end of a state to the other. The truth is that it's a negotiable item between buyers and sellers. We always put in our offers that the sellers pay for title insurance with the rationale that they can't expect us to buy unless they are willing to prove that they have the right to sell. It also gives us another negotiating pawn to use.

Is it important to pay for title insurance? What if you are paying cash for the property, and nobody is insisting on it?

Always get title insurance. It protects you against a myriad of things that could affect your ownership of the property. Someone might show up claiming to have a lien on the property. A relative of the seller could make a claim that the sellers didn't have the right to sell it to you. There could be restrictions on use. There could be tax liens. There could be encroachments on the property, or you could have structures encroaching on other people's property. Strangely enough, it doesn't protect you against the one thing that you would assume it would protect against: On most policies, the title company doesn't physically inspect the property. Your dream home could be underwater for all the company knows, or it could have blown into the next county during a hurricane, and you're not protected against that by title insurance. Title insurance protects your title to the land (the dirt) but not the structures on the property.

I live in Texas. Are there certain contracts that have to be used for Texas?

We believe most states are similar these days. Most boards of Realtors have an approved contract, but this doesn't mean that it has to be used. We've written deals on a legal pad before and closed on them. Think of an offer as a preliminary understanding that will be replaced by a legal contract later that will be created by an attorney or an escrow officer depending on the custom in your state. The preliminary agreement could be as loose as, "Buyer to buy! Seller to sell! Details to follow in a contract."

When do you ask for seller financing?

Just about all the time because it can give you so much more flexibility. Don't get caught up in the 20 percent down, 80 percent bank financing quagmire when it comes to real estate. Don't be afraid to ask for seller financing. There is a ton of it available for the asking.

Do you recommend putting a "weasel clause" into the offer so that you can get your deposit back if you change your mind?

"Weasel clauses" are contingencies put in a real estate contract so that the buyer has a way out of the contract. We've never worried too much about weasel clauses. If you put up a $500 deposit, that's usually the extent of your potential loss in the event you decide to back out. Many new investors don't understand this. They think that if they get an offer accepted, they are legally bound to buy the property. Not so. All you're risking is the earnest-money deposit. You might even think of it as an option to buy that you have just paid for.

In your 0 percent interest seller carry-back offers, do you ever have an annual payment plan versus monthly, such as $10,000 in year 1, $10,000 in year 3, and $10,000 in year 5?

We usually ask for regular monthly payments for cash-flow purposes, but quarterly or annual payments work just as well. It's easier to get the seller's approval of terms that are structured in a more conventional manner. If it's new to the seller, he or she might get nervous. Quarterly, semiannual, or annual terms usually are requested by the seller rather than offered by us. Perhaps they have a child going into college, and they would prefer a lump sum each September to pay their child's college tuition, for example. Other requirements also may lead sellers to request atypical payment arrangements.

I have a partner, and we are about to buy our first property. My partner really likes interest-only loans, especially because they lower our mortgage payments. I was wondering about your thoughts on the subject. Are interest-only loans good for investors, or is it best to stick with more traditional mortgages?

Your question about interest-only loans is a good one. We don't have strong feelings one way or another about using interest-only loans. A lot depends on why you are using them. If it's to lower payments and improve cash flow, we'd prefer to use more conventional financing because the loan is paying down while appreciation pushes the value up. You build equity much quicker this way. When you're just starting, interest-only loans are more attractive than they will be once you begin building some significant cash flow. If you have to use interest-only financing in the beginning, we'd recommend that you move to an amortizing loan as quickly as possible. The faster you build equity and net worth, the easier it will be to finance new purchases. Banks like to see you paying off loans.

Is there an Internet site you would recommend to calculate the interest rates, etc. you speak about in your book? I purchased a fairly expensive financial calculator but have had constant problems with it.

We can understand your problems with some of the financial calculators on the market. Many of them can be difficult to use. This is why we recommend the one in Carleton Sheets' Real Estate Toolkit. This is a program that comes on CD that you load on your computer. It not only has a great financial calculator (the one used to run all the calculations in our books), but there are also numerous other tools you will need as you get started investing. The best part is that it's simple to use. Just log on to our Web site (weekendmillionaire.com), and you will find a link on the home page where you can order the toolkit.

27

Nothing-Down
Deals That Work

Much has been written and spoken about buying property with no money down. No doubt it's a great concept, and it can work. What could be better that to take title to an asset without having to put any of your own money into it and then have it earn enough to pay for itself?

There are dozens, maybe even scores, of books, tapes, CDs, and seminars on how to buy with no money down, but they don't tell you much about how to own the properties after you buy them. They assume that if you can just buy them, someone will come along and buy them from you for even more. Our experience is just the opposite; we find that most of the properties you can buy for no money down, you can't afford to own after you buy them.

This is the reason we titled this chapter "Nothing-Down Deals That Work," with the emphasis being on the word "work." Yes, we've bought properties with no money down, but for every one we purchased, we chose not to purchase dozens that we could have bought that way.

Our readers have many differing views on the no-money-down concept, and the following questions reflect this.

How to Structure the Offer

My real estate club members all tell me that I should use a mortgage broker and not use my own money if at all possible. Will a mortgage broker be able to help me make no-money-down deals better than going directly to the bank?

If you can deal directly with the lenders, that's your best bet. Mortgage brokers provide a service, but they take a percentage for putting the deals together. One big advantage of using a mortgage broker is that the broker may have access to sources of unconventional financing that may be less skeptical about providing financing to buyers who are not putting any of their own money at risk.

Don't conventional lenders require 20 percent down? How can you make no-money-down deals if you have to put that much cash into them?

No money down doesn't mean that there is no cash involved. It just means that you don't put *your* cash into the deal. When we use conventional lenders to make no-money-down deals, we typically obtain a small first mortgage from the lender (20 to 50 percent) and then get the balance of the money through seller financing or third-party private lenders. The funds from the small first mortgage can go to pay off mortgage balances, to pay real estate commissions, or simply to give the seller some cash. If you aren't happy with the rates or terms you get on such a transaction after you own the property for a year, you usually can get a higher-percentage loan from a conventional lender and still end up with a fully financed purchase. Just make sure that in any situation your no-money-down deals will generate cash flow.

Banks usually will let you finance only about four properties through them, correct? Then do you have to go from one bank to another to buy more, or do you need to find private lenders?

You are probably talking about what are referred to as "qualifying loans," loans that will qualify for federal insurance, can be sold on the secondary market, and are not considered active investor loans. Currently, the number of such loans one borrower can have is 10, and it doesn't matter whether they are all with one bank or with several banks. Once you get above this number, your loans are considered active investor loans and are classified differently and scrutinized more carefully by federal bank examiners. A bank can make you as many loans as it wants; it's just that when you get more than 10, they are looked at differently and aren't sold on the secondary market.

What about buying properties subject to existing financing and getting the sellers to carry back the balance? Is this a good way to make no-money-down deals?

Twenty years ago that was how most no-money-down deals were made, but today you need to be careful about buying properties subject to existing financing. Most underlying loans today have an acceleration clause in the event of a sale. Some people will tell you that you can just ignore this clause because as long as the lender is getting paid, it doesn't care. The problem is that the lenders *do* care, and there are many risks associated with such transactions. Our recommendation is that if you want to assume the underlying financing, inform the lender and get permission. Veterans Administration (VA) and Federal Housing Authority (FHA) loans are still assumable, but you have to go through an assumption process and pay a small fee. If you're looking to buy and hold a property for the income stream, the last thing you want is for the lender to call the loan soon after you have purchased the property.

What is the best source of financing for no-money-down deals?

So much time is devoted to discussing institutional lenders, but a huge percentage of real estate sales are financed by the sellers or by third-party individuals. There is a world of opportunity out there when you are dealing with sellers who have a low mortgage or own the property free and clear. Don't be afraid to ask sellers to finance part or all of the purchase, and don't overlook the fact that there are individuals with money looking for a place to invest it other than the stock market.

If you have purchased a property subject to an existing loan and you make the payments as called for, why would the lender attempt to call the loan even if this did technically violate the terms of the loan agreement?

Aside from it possibly being considered fraud, let's look at a very specific reason. Assume that the interest rate on the loan is 6 percent, and since the loan was originally made, the prevailing rates have gone to 10 percent. If the lender finds out that you have violated the terms of the loan by transferring the property, don't you think the bank would have plenty of incentive to call the note so that it could put the money to work at the higher rate? Often when a lender exercises the due-on-sale clause, it doesn't necessarily mean that it wants to be paid off; it may only mean it wants to charge you points for transferring the loan, or it wants to increase the interest rate. Either of these can hurt your cash flow.

If you buy a property "subject to" and do it legally, do you call the lender in advance to find out what the requirements will be to assume the loan? I have been told that you can get around the "due on sale" clause by using a living trust and/or a corporation. Which is correct, or are both correct?

Mike has assumed several loans that had "due on sale" clauses, but his credit is impeccable, and in most cases, the bank would rather have him on the loan than the person it had before. He will not, however, buy properties "subject to" existing loans and try to use some gimmick such as a trust or other entity to deceive the lenders. In our opinion, a "due on sale" clause is just that, and trying to circumvent it without the lender's knowledge is wrong.

How can you buy a property for no money down when the seller wants at least some cash?

A great no-money-down technique is to get a small (20 to 40 percent) first mortgage, which provides money for you to give the sellers some cash, and then ask the seller to finance the balance. In this way the seller gets cash, but it's not your cash. Since the seller is getting the money from the first mortgage, even if the buyer defaults on the first mortgage and the seller has to pay the loan off, it would be no different than if the seller had borrowed the money himself or herself. The seller simply pays it back and ends up with the property back. We realize that this sounds simple, but there are some risks that sellers take when they make a deal such as this, so your job is to make them feel comfortable that you will be able to perform on the loans.

Is it really possible to buy properties when you have no money to put down?

Just because you don't put up any money doesn't mean that the seller doesn't get some cash. Remember that sellers can get money out by putting a first mortgage on the property. Your note to them is in second position, but you have to be careful. Read the chapter in our book about nothing-down deals that work. The reason we say be careful is because it is easy to buy properties with no money down that you can't afford to own after you buy them. Don't be afraid to ask for 0 percent financing from owners. All they can do is either say no or counter with a request for some interest rate on the loan. See the answer to the preceding question.

Is there enough property owned free and clear to make it worthwhile trying to get seller financing?

A huge amount of real estate in America is owned free and clear, and we're not just talking about single-family homes; we're also talking about all real estate. If this is the case, opportunities should abound. The biggest obstacle to getting seller financing is the failure to ask for it.

I've been making offers in Florida for the past four months, and no one wants to do financing with or without interest. I have offered 6 to 10 percent more than the asking price, and still no one has showed any interest. They want their money now. How do you make the seller feel comfortable with owner financing? All I get is, "How do I know you are not going to trash the place and default on the note?"

There are some people who can sell ice water to Eskimos and others who couldn't sell $20 bills for $10. Why? How you present yourself and how you present your offers have everything to do with whether or not sellers will want to deal with you. If you look and act as though you're insecure and unsure of what you're doing, sellers aren't going to feel very comfortable about dealing with you—keep in mind that you are asking them to loan you a substantial amount of money. The more professional you look, the more trustworthy you come across, and the better track record of success you can show them, the easier it is to get seller financing.

If you give the sellers a 10 or 20 percent down payment, wouldn't they be more inclined to finance the rest of the purchase price?

When you put some of your money into a deal, both sellers and banks are more comfortable making you a loan. Also, seller financing and bank financing get easier to obtain when you have a track record; until then, you have to do a sales job.

Let's be honest about no-money-down purchases. How do you find them, and how often can you make them work?

We find very few true no-money-down deals that will work for the long-term investor. There are plenty of no-money-down deals that won't work. There's never been a problem finding properties that can be bought for no money down that you can't afford to own once you buy them. Our recommendation is to calculate the net operating income (NOI) for a property and then structure your no-money-down offers so that they will work with that NOI. This is the only way that we know to make them work.

I've been researching how to get started in real estate investing, and I've learned that the most important step in getting started is to start! *In other words, do* something. *I've familiarized myself with my area, home prices, and rental prices; found a couple of buyers' brokers; identified about a dozen good mortgage sources; and have a couple of property management companies to choose from. My problem is that I estimate that I'll need about $40,000 to get started. I've heard that for a beginning investor (with no track record), it may be difficult to get a mortgage for more than 80 percent of a purchase (unless the purchase price is* dramatically *below market value). So this means that in my area, a $125,000 property would require about a $25,000 down payment. In addition to the down payment, I'm estimating (on the high side) $5,000 for closing costs, $5,000 for "startup expenses" such as legal and accounting, and I'd want to have about a $5,000 buffer to cover vacancies and unexpected expenses. These total $40,000. Now I probably can scrape together a few thousand dollars if I* *really try hard, but putting together $40,000 would take me years. How do I put together this kind of cash in a relatively short period of time without much free time to do it? Or are my numbers and expectations unrealistic?*

You've asked one of the best questions yet! You're not unlike thousands of other people who feel that they need a lot of money to get started. You don't! What you're referring to in your comment is conventional bank financing. There are many sources of financing other than banks. We cover several ways to buy property without bank financing in *The Weekend Millionaire's Secrets to Investing in Real Estate*. The most logical source is owner financing, which is used very frequently. Private third-party financing is also an excellent source of funds. In Chapter 27 of the book we describe a purchase Mike made using a combination of private third-party financing and zero-interest owner financing that not only didn't require any cash down but also netted him $20,000 cash at closing. Try reading Chapters 25, 26, and 27 of the real estate book; they will help you to understand this concept better.

I have just returned from an overseas assignment and have been planning on learning all I can about real estate investing. I am always willing to learn more. I am very anxious to begin investing as a career. I was wondering if there are any known "strategies" or pointers I could employ using a Veterans Administration (VA) loan to sort of kick-start my investments?

You can use your VA loan eligibility to purchase a house in which to live, and we understand that after the first year, you could then rent it out. There is a penalty if you get caught using your VA loan to buy investment properties. Another problem is that even if you live in it for a year before renting it, until you sell or refinance the property with a conventional loan, you can't reestablish your eligibility to obtain another VA loan. If you have some money saved and can afford to go conventional, we'd recommend that before tying up your VA eligibility. Incidentally, "VA loan" is a misnomer. The loan is made by a conventional lender, and the VA merely guarantees the loan. There is no maximum, but in practice, the maximum loan tends to be the amount of loan the lender can sell in the secondary market.

28

Tax Benefits
of Owning
Real Estate

One of the big advantages of owning real estate is the favorable tax treatment you get on the income it produces. The money you borrow to buy a car, boat, or recreational vehicle, and even the money you owe on your credit cards, all costs you interest. This interest buys you nothing other than the opportunity to get what you want a little quicker. You can't even deduct the interest on your tax return.

Real estate is different. When you borrow money to purchase real estate that you will hold for rent, not only can you deduct the interest against the rental income you receive, but you also can deduct a portion of the value of the structure as well. That is called "depreciation." The income you receive in the form of rent is not subject to self-employment taxes, and in many cases you can defer or avoid paying tax on the gain when you sell the property. Even if you are taxed on the profits you make from a sale, provided that you have owned the property for at least a year, your profit is taxed at a much more favorable capital gains rate instead of the ordinary income rate. Real estate gives you all these advantages, and in addition, while you own the property, you can deduct the cost of any repairs, taxes, insurance, or other expenses you incur.

Naturally, with all these tax advantages to owning real estate, it is going to produce questions. One of the problems we have with answering these questions is the fact that we are not professional tax advisors. The answers we provide in this chapter should not be relied on in preparing your tax returns, and we strongly urge you to seek the advice of a tax attorney or CPA to confirm any deductions or other favorable tax advantages you plan to use.

I have several thousand dollars in a 401(k) sitting in a low-interest bank account. I am thinking about buying a property using that money to buy it for cash, taking about a month and a half to rehab it, and then refinancing it immediately *after that to get all my money back. Then the tenant can pay the mortgage. Is that a smart move, or should I look for financing elsewhere right from the start?*

This is a question for a good tax advisor. We think that you can borrow from your 401(k) to do this, but you have to return the money to the account within 60 days to avoid having to declare it as income. We urge you to verify this with your CPA or tax attorney. If you can use your 401(k) money, and it's only for a month or two, we'd suggest that you do so. If you're going to have to refinance after completing the renovations anyway, there's not much point in trying to get a new loan for such a short time—plus it's quite expensive. If you can get a new loan in the beginning for enough to do the rehab work, that could be another option, but you probably would have payments to make until you rented it that you would not have if you used your own money.

I'll be closing on a house in early December, and I will need to rehab it before I can rent it. Should I try to cram in as much of the rehab work as possible before the end of the year in order to get the tax deductions?

It all depends on your tax situation; if you need the deductions in the current year, by all means do as much of the work as possible and pay for it before year end. On the other hand, if you don't need the deductions, you always can start the work and get as much done as possible but wait until after the first of the year to pay for it, thereby deferring the deductions until the next tax year.

How to Structure the Offer

Can I deduct both materials and labor for the rehab work, or can I only deduct the cost of the materials?

There's no question that you can deduct the cost of materials. Labor is another thing; if it's other people's labor that your are paying for, you can deduct it, but if it's your labor, you probably can't unless the property is held in a separate tax entity and that entity writes you a check for your labor. If you deducted your labor, you also would have to show it as income to you, so it would be a wash. It would be nice to take a big tax deduction for our labor and not have to report any income for it. We would never pay any tax if this were allowed!

Can I write a big check to a supplier such as Home Depot or Lowe's, for example, deduct the expense for materials in this tax year, and draw against the credit next year?

This is another one of those question that you need to take up with your tax advisor, but our gut reaction is no. You may be able to get away with prepaying for a specific item but not setting up an account. The government allows so many favorable tax treatments for real estate that we can't see them looking favorably on a scheme such as this, but check with your CPA or tax attorney.

I am speculating on a condo in Treasure Island, Florida, that I have a reserved bid on for $214,000. Now I've learned that St. Pete's beach is literally exploding with growth and that new condo developments are popping up over a five-mile length down the beach with an average price of beachfront units running at $290,000. It will show a negative cash flow (I know . . . I know . . . I have read your book!), but I can still make a profit, can't I?

Speculating on beach condos violates several of the "14 Biggest Mistakes New Investors Make." Reread Chapter 40 in *The Weekend Millionaire's Secrets to Investing in Real Estate* and Chapter 32 of this book. A lot of people have made money doing just what you are talking about, but there are many more who have lost their shirts. We know because dozens of them

174

have come to us offering great deals just to get rid of the condos and get out from under the negative cash flow.

In Chapter 28 of The Weekend Millionaire's Secrets to Investing in Real Estate, *it states that the long-term capital gains rate for federal income tax is 20 percent. Wasn't that was changed effective May 6, 2003, to 15 percent for most taxpayers?*

Yes, we understand the capital gains rate was changed, and it may change again before this book is published. This is just another reason that you should consult a good tax attorney or CPA instead of relying solely on what you read here. Tax laws change almost every year, and it is the job of these paid professionals to keep up with the changes.

Is it true that I can make as much as I want renting properties and not have to pay Social Security taxes?

Yes, FICA taxes are paid on earned income, not passive or investment income. There is currently a maximum amount on which these taxes are paid, and whatever you pay, your employer is required to match. If you are self-employed, you have to pay not only the employee portion but also the employer portion of these taxes too. In many cases this totals more than your total income tax liability. When your income comes from rents, you can earn as much as you want and never have to pay these taxes. This is another big reason that real estate is such a great investment.

Why does the Internal Revenue Service let you take depreciation on rental properties but not on your home?

Rental properties receive much the same treatment as business equipment for tax purposes. When companies buy equipment to use in the operation of the business, the assumption is that the equipment eventually will wear out and have to be replaced; therefore, each year the companies are allowed to take a deduction for the estimated amount of value the equipment loses in that year. The number of years over which various kinds of equipment may be depreciated is established by the IRS and varies based on its estimated life. Naturally, real estate, with its long life, must be depreciated over a greater number of years than a computer that may be obsolete in 3 to 5 years. Currently, residential properties such as houses and apartments may be depreciated over 27.5 years and commercial properties over 39 years. Like everything else about the tax code, depreciation schedules are subject to change, so check with your tax attorney or CPA for the rules currently in effect.

PART VI

Moving into Larger Properties

We strongly believe that as new investors you should start small, with single-family homes. In the beginning, when your knowledge and experience are limited, single-family homes provide the safest and most secure real estate investments. Once you have acquired a number of single-family homes, have experienced the ups and downs of being a landlord, and have cash flow from your investments, you may want to look into buying larger properties such as apartment buildings and commercial properties. This seems to be a natural progression for conservative real estate investors and one that we took ourselves.

In this part of *The Weekend Millionaire's Secrets to Investing in Real Estate* we discussed investing in multifamily and commercial properties but also included a chapter on what we feel is the most important thing you need to do when moving into larger properties—and that is building a support team.

The differences between investing in these larger properties and investing in single-family homes are so great that surrounding yourself with a group of competent professionals is imperative. The management requirements, accounting, financial, tax, and other treatments are much more complicated and risky for apartments and commercial properties than they are for single-family homes.

As with most types of investments, greater risks bring the potential for higher returns, and apartments and commercial properties are no different. We don't want to discourage anyone from investing in larger properties. What we want you to do is to move into them slowly and with your eyes open. Just as the top stock car drivers on NASCAR's Nextel Cup Series didn't start in this top division, you shouldn't try to start your real estate investing career on top either. Most of them started at small local tracks and gradually worked their way up through divisions in which increasing competition and skill levels enabled them to improve and hone their skills until they were ready for the top division.

This part of our real estate book was designed simply to make you aware of the greater opportunities and to encourage you to build your knowledge and hone your skills until you are ready to jump into the big leagues.

29

Valuing Multifamily Properties

Throughout *The Weekend Millionaire's Secrets to Investing in Real Estate* we stress the importance of new investors starting with single-family homes. We know that it is much harder to buy houses using the Weekend Millionaire methods owing to competition from homeowners, but it is a safe and sure way to get started without taking unnecessary risks. By starting slowly and gaining experience, you prepare yourself to move eventually into multifamily properties with the knowledge required to be successful.

Renting single-family homes is very simple compared with apartments. The expenses associated with renting single-family homes are minimal and, with few exceptions, are limited to management, maintenance reserve, taxes, and insurance. These expenses are fairly easy to calculate and use to determine net operating income (NOI). Apartments, on the other hand, have expenses for common-area maintenance, utilities, recreational amenities, grounds maintenance, and many other things not associated with single-family homes. Vacancies are often higher, quality of tenants lower, and turnover expenses higher with apartments than with single-family homes. Calculating NOI for apartment buildings is more of a science.

For these reasons, we feel that it is critical for a new investor to either have very deep pockets or gain adequate experience before moving into apartments. If you start with single-family homes and are having problems there, they will be compounded by moving into these larger properties. Buying and renting single-family homes allows new investors to test the waters before taking the plunge. Following are questions we have been asked about investing in apartment buildings.

I'm a new investor and plan to start with single-family residences. Then I want get into larger properties. How long should I wait until I move into multifamily units?

Time is not as important as experience. We recommend that you make several purchases of single-family homes and operate them as rentals before moving into multifamily properties. Some people can do this in a couple of years; others may take five years or more. What's important is that you learn the business by buying and owning rental houses before you start getting into larger units. We'd recommend that you buy 5 to 10 single-family homes before moving into multifamily or commercial properties. This will give you good experience and the opportunity to build some cash flow before buying one of the larger properties. Once you start looking for multifamily properties, try to limit yourself to ones for which the dollar value won't be more than 30 percent of the value of your overall investment portfolio. Keep in mind that when you get into larger properties, there are many things to deal with that aren't there in single-family homes, things such as common-area maintenance, utilities, etc.

I would like to bring in a partner to purchase a four-unit building. How do I structure the deal to buy him out within five years?

It's hard to give a short answer to this question. First, why is a partnership necessary? Is it because you fear doing it alone? If so, think again; equal partnerships are a most difficult way to do business because neither side has a controlling interest. Be overly cautious and enter the arrangement knowing that at least half of all partnerships (like marriages) end up in trouble.

Valuing Multifamily Properties

With that said, perhaps you can agree on a buyout price when you set up the partnership. If not, you can offer to have the property appraised and then give your partner the option to either buy your interest or sell you his at some agreed-on future date for one-half the appraised value. If he still won't agree to this arrangement, offer to give him the same buy/sell offer at 55 percent of the appraised value. Don't forget to look into the tax consequences for both sides. How you do it might make a difference in how much you have to pay. If, for example, the other partner has capital losses from other investments that were sold for a loss, he or she might prefer to sell and let the capital gain be offset by the losses carrying forward. If he or she has a lot of depreciation allowance, it might be more advantageous to buy and receive rent that could be offset with the depreciation allowance. Reaching agreements in advance to dissolve partnerships is sort of like drafting prenuptial agreements; they usually require professional help to structure fairly.

In The Weekend Millionaire's Secrets to Investing in Real Estate *you recommend single-family homes as the best initial investments. Since the prices per unit for them are so high in relation to commercial or multifamily properties, what are your thoughts on condominiums?*

We don't like condominiums because there are too many variables that you can't control. These include homeowners' fees, changing regulations that could prohibit you from renting, and other restrictions on the use of your property. While the developer is still in control, you don't have to worry too much about this, but once the developer has sold out the project and moved on, a homeowners' association takes control. Note that these are called "homeowners' associations," not real estate investors' associations. Often the developer has kept the homeowners' fees artificially low to make the project look more attractive, and one of the first things the new association learns is that the fees have to be raised immediately to cover expenses. This, in effect, gives the association the right to tax you by raising homeowners' dues. The bylaws of most condo associations also give them the right to amend the declarations, even to the point of restricting your right to rent the units. These are just a few of the reasons we don't like condos.

Moving into Larger Properties

I've been working on deals to buy entire portfolios from old investors who just want to cash out and go live on an island or something. I've got some very interesting deals. One is for about $8 million worth of properties. I will look for folks who want to buy a piece of this because it is bigger than I can reasonably do myself. Any cautions to offer?

Be very cautious, and take the time to inspect each property carefully. Our experience with buying large blocks of properties from other investors is that often they have been pulling money out for years without reserving for deferred maintenance. Suddenly they find themselves in a position where the properties need new roofs, new heating and air-conditioning systems, new carpet, and new paint, and they don't have the money to do the work. This is usually why they are looking to sell rather than wanting to go live on an island somewhere. You need to be especially careful in these situations because the seller's records usually show the properties to be very profitable. This is because the seller hasn't been keeping up with the maintenance.

I looked at a two-family flat today that needs about $15,000 worth of work. Should I get it appraised first, do the work, and get the second appraisal?

What do you plan to do with the appraisals? Appraisals are for banks. They won't tell you anything about whether or not you are getting a good deal. The only way to do that is run the numbers like we show you in *The Weekend Millionaire's Secrets to Investing in Real Estate* and then see if you can buy with the net operating income (NOI). Run the numbers based on what the property will bring after you fix it up. Value it based on these numbers, and then subtract the amount it will take for repairs. This will tell you what to offer for the property.

I am itching to buy a larger complex for the cash flow and to use it as a springboard for becoming a full-time investor. Are the risks really that much greater than starting with single-family homes?

Yes, you can get great cash flow with bigger complexes, but we advise you to learn the business with single-family homes because there is that much difference between them and the bigger properties. We have a friend who was doing quite well with single-family homes, so he bought a 20-unit building using the same formulas he used to buy the single-family homes. Within a year, the 20-unit complex was consuming all his cash flow from the single-family homes plus additional money from his salary. He told us that the second happiest day of his life was the day he closed on the purchase of the 20-unit building but that the happiest was the day he sold it. He learned the difference between single-family homes and apartments the hard way.

I own five single-family homes, and I think I am ready to take the risk of buying an apartment building. Any suggestions about what I should look for?

Buying larger units is not about the risk . . . it's about experience. Things can happen with larger properties that can sink you, but with a little experience, you can avoid the pitfalls. We suggest that you look for sound buildings in good areas, but ones that don't have much pizzazz. You'd be amazed how a building can go up in value and become more appealing to renters when you add a false roof and some eye-catching details that you can do very cheaply. We'd also recommend that you start small. Buy a 4- to 6-unit building in order to get the feel for investing in apartments before you look at 20- to 40-unit complexes. A small 4- to 6-unit building can let you see the difference in quality of tenants you get with apartments versus houses and let you experience the added costs of a multifamily property without taking too big a risk. Once you gain experience with a small multifamily building, it will make the transition to larger buildings easier.

I'm looking at 10 units in a great location. One is a quad, and one has six units. I talked with the owner, and he wanted to know if I was a broker. When I said no, he lost interest in talking to me. I'm thinking he wants to put a lot of the money in his pocket. Do you agree with that?

Don't assume anything. If you're interested in the properties and feel that you are ready to make the jump to multifamily units, make him an offer. His seeming loss of interest may be nothing more than him thinking that you aren't a serious prospect or capable of buying.

I'm going to a bankruptcy auction that is a very hostile environment. The current owner won't give the bank the rent rolls or operating expenses for the property. The auctioneer has what he calls "unofficial" rents, and I'm using 35 percent for expenses and 5 percent as a vacancy factor. I'm trying to back into a price to offer at the auction and was wondering what else I should factor into the decision? The properties were renovated within the last two years, separate meters, in a very strong rental area.

We recommend that you do your homework first; calculate the rents and vacancies based on local market conditions, and make your offer based on what the property should be able to do rather than what a seller in distress or a bank wanting to unload it says it will do. Have you been able to talk to the bank officer handling the bankruptcy situation? Sometimes bank officers have more information than you can get from the auctioneer, and we find that they are usually more forthcoming with information because they fear repercussions if they misrepresent what they know. No matter what the property was doing in the past, it's what you plan to do with it in the future that should determine what you want to pay for it.

When buying apartment units, how do you account for vacancy? As an example, let's assume 34 units with 10 vacancies. Do you run your numbers on actual rent roll and operating expenses?

We try to be conservative with the vacancy factors we use when computing net operating income (NOI). Every market is different, and conditions within a given market are constantly changing, so we'd suggest that you conduct your own research about what the vacancy is for your market and then use a factor 1 to 2 percent higher in your NOI calculations. If the actual vacancy is better than what you used in your calculations, that translates into better cash flow and more money in your pocket. If you miss the other way, it means less cash flow and more money out of your pocket. Better to be conservative and miss a purchase than to stretch it just to make the deal look good and then have it become an "alligator." However, projecting 10 vacancies for 34 seems very conservative to us. You very likely may be able to keep 90 percent of them rented.

If a complex has high vacancies but the area is good, what would be one way to negotiate great terms?

Valuing Multifamily Properties

If the seller gives you the actual vacancy rate for the past year or two and it is more than you estimated it would be, dwell on the high vacancy numbers, and use them as a reason to ask for favorable terms. Tell the seller that you need better terms in order to give you time to correct the problem. Tell the seller that your bank doesn't want to put much of a loan on the property because of the history of high vacancies, but you would like to buy the property if he or she will finance a good portion of the purchase price. There are many similar angles you can use when asking for discount seller financing using the high vacancy as your reason for the request.

What about building a multifamily property versus buying an existing one?

One problem with building is that you have the construction time where you have to pay interest on construction financing but are getting no rent. Development is a specialized art, but if you really know what you're doing and know how to do it well, you often can build for considerably less than you can buy. One caution: In a booming market, rising prices take care of mistakes, but when the market flattens out, you can really get hurt.

I see a lot of advertisements for condominium presales. Are these worthwhile investments?

We recommend that you stay away from the condo presales. Condos tend not to be good investments for long-term rentals, and the presales often are nothing more than a developer's way of raising capital during construction. Developers can paint rosy pictures, but their entire sales pitch usually centers on how much profit you can make when you sell. There is too much uncertainty for long-term investors. We view this as speculating, not investing.

What about prebuying single-family homes? I mean buying from the developer before he starts construction?

Once again, we view this as speculating, not investing. There are people in California and Florida making some big bucks buying preconstruction houses because prices have been going up significantly before they have to put any serious money into them. While there are some who are making a profit, there is a substantial risk involved because the market could go down in value before the project is finished. While we don't recommend it, if you're determined to speculate, and if you can put up only a couple of thousand dollars deposit when you sign a contract, you always could choose to walk away from the deal and lose your $2,000 if the market drops. It would be similar to paying $2,000 for an option to buy and then choosing not to exercise the option.

I'm planning to purchase a duplex or fourplex, move into one of the apartments, and let one or three other people pay off most of my expenses and mortgage. My question is: How do I use the equation from your book to calculate my net operating income (NOI)?

Just compute the NOI the way we show you in Chapter 5 of *The Weekend Millionaire's Secrets to Investing in Real Estate,* and use this calculation to compute the value of the property. It will be very hard to rent one unit of a duplex for enough to pay for both units in the building, but you may be able to come close with a four-unit building. Even if you can't rent the other units for enough to entirely pay for your unit, so what? You're going to have to pay rent or a house payment to live somewhere. Why not just look at the portion you have to come up with to make the deal work as your cost of living?

What are your thoughts about investing in condos in downtown areas (Chicago, for example)? As long as you follow the traditional rules and purchase to make a cash flow, isn't there less risk just because the condo association takes care of maintenance/repair problems, which isn't the case with a single-family house? As long as the building is being fairly well maintained and the entry price of the condo is close to what we can finance, wouldn't this make sense?

We've had several questions about condos, so we want to start by saying that not all condos are bad investments. Your point about the condo association taking care of maintenance/repair problems is one of the reasons that we say you need to be careful about investing in condos. When you buy a condo, you become part of the association that has to take care of the problems, and the more problems there are, the higher your monthly dues go. For anyone looking to buy in a condominium complex, either as an investment property or as a place to live, pay attention to deferred maintenance. Then obtain a copy of the association's financial statement and see how much money has been reserved to cover these expenses. If the roofs need replacing, buildings need painting, or parking needs repaving, stay away from the project unless the association has the money set aside to do the work. You can bet that the owners are about to be hit with a big assessment.

30

Valuing Commercial Properties

There are wonderful opportunities in commercial properties for people with the knowledge and courage to invest in them. Unlike single-family homes that are fairly straightforward investments, commercial properties are not for the faint of heart. For example, if a single-family home has a vacancy; it often can be filled in a matter of days. A commercial property can take months or even years to find a tenant. In some cases commercial buildings may have to be demolished and rebuilt before the property becomes marketable.

Many new investors have a little success with a couple of single-family homes and even some apartment buildings and then allow their exuberance to propel them into commercial investments before they are ready. When this happens, they often lose not only the commercial property but also the residential properties that were bringing them success.

What is the difference between multifamily property and commercial property?

Valuing Commercial Properties

"Multifamily property" usually refers to apartment buildings containing four or more units. "Commercial property" refers to retail locations, shopping centers, storage buildings such as warehouses or self-storage projects, manufacturing sites, and mobile home parks. Commercial real estate investing is a completely different world. Don't try it until you are successful buying rental houses and multifamily properties. Finding the right tenant who is financially sound is difficult, and you may have to put up a lot of cash to remodel the property to the tenant's needs. Commercial investing also tends to be feast or famine. If you own 10 rental houses, you can afford to have one of them vacant at any time. If you own one large commercial building and lose your tenant or can't find one, you have no income coming in and may have to spend a lot of money finding one.

How difficult is it to finance commercial property? I have heard that you need to put 25 to 30 percent down.

That all depends! Commercial lending decisions are made on a case-by-case basis and often rely on the creditworthiness of the tenant rather than the investor. This is one of the reasons why a new investor should learn the business by investing in single-family residences first. Lenders are comfortable lending on houses and have a formula in place. They know that houses and even small apartments are very marketable to a wide segment of the population, whereas commercial lending is much more complicated. With a solid-credit tenant, you might be able to get 100 percent financing on a commercial property, but with speculative commercial investments, you may have to come up with 50 percent down or more to finance them.

How big does a project have to be for cash flow to determine market value instead of emotion?

We value all properties based on cash flow, even though banks tend to look at comparison-market-value appraisals more when financing single-family homes. We think that anything larger than a single-family home is a business deal unless it's two- to four-unit buildings and the buyer intends to live in one of the units. Even if the owner lives in a four-unit building, the price still could be affected by emotion, but this is an exception rather than a rule. Emotion often causes individuals to pay too much for single-family homes, but investors tend to run the numbers and price their deals strictly on cash flow. You aren't usually competing with people who want to live in the property when you buy apartment buildings and commercial properties.

When purchasing mobile home parks, would you recommend purchasing parks where the mobile homes are park-owned or where there are only pads to rent out?

We wouldn't consider a park where we owned the mobile homes. Mobile homes go down in value. Only the individual pads and the park go up in value. Just buy the land and let the tenants take the depreciation on the homes. The real estate company that Roger ran in Los Angeles once had a lucrative business buying trashy mobile homes in order to take over the lease on the space. Shortage of spaces for mobile homes is a big problem in big cities. The company sold the trashy mobile homes in Arizona and put a new mobile home into the old space, making profit on the sale of the new home. Investing in mobile home parks is a specialized business. While owning the land and pads is very simple, we'd urge you to stay away from owning the mobile homes unless you really understand the business and know how to protect yourself. Always remember the underlying principle involved: Mobile homes almost always go down in value, but owning the pads or the park is profitable.

What is meant by the term "net lease" investment?

A "net lease" is one in which the expenses are paid by the tenant, and the money the owner gets is net to him or her. These are used primarily with commercial properties and can be expanded to what are called "triple net leases," in which the tenant pays all the big three expenses: taxes, insurance, and maintenance. In some parts of the country this is called an "absolute net lease." A triple net lease tends to favor the Lessor because expenses are variable and almost always go up, not down. In some cases tenants might negotiate a net lease "with caps" in order to limit their exposure, but these types of commercial leases are rare. In other cases the Lessor may pay the taxes and insurance, with the tenant agreeing to pay any increases in these expenses over the most recent year's expense.

Valuing Commercial Properties

Who pays the maintenance where you have common areas that must be maintained and the expenses are prorated among several tenants?

These are often handled by adding common-area maintenance (CAM) fees to the lease rate. When this is done, the CAM fee often is recalculated periodically to reflect actual costs based on historical expenses. For example, a shopping center with 100,000 square feet and an annual CAM expense of $300,000 could add $3.00 per square foot of space rented. If the CAM expense increases to $350,000 annually, the CAM fee may be increased to $3.50 per square foot.

Is there such thing as a "gross lease" in which the Lessor pays all expenses?

Absolutely! When dealing with commercial leases, the Lessor and Lessee can agree to virtually any type of arrangement they want. This is one of the big differences between commercial and residential leases. In most states, the terms of residential leases are restricted by landlord/tenant laws that do not apply to commercial leases. As you can see, leasing commercial property is very different from renting houses, and the terms of the leases generally are the product of negotiations between the Lessor and the Lessee.

We own a small building in the center of our little town and are having difficulty selling it. After reading The Weekend Millionaire's Secrets to Investing in Real Estate, *we started wondering if in the long run we wouldn't be smarter to lease it instead. What do you think?*

We are believers in buying and holding. That's the basis of the Weekend Millionaire investing strategy. About the only time we would recommend selling is if you really need to get the cash out of the investment or if the neighborhood is declining rapidly and you can't see it being revitalized any time soon.

When leasing commercial properties, is it customary for the Lessor or the Lessee to pay for renovations to make a property ready for the tenant?

Anything goes when leasing commercial properties. In some cases the Lessor will lease the bare space, and the tenant will put in all of his or her improvements; in other cases the Lessor will do all the improvements; and in others the tenant will be given an allowance for improvements and then have to pay increased rental if the improvements go over this allowance. Virtually any arrangements can be negotiated between the parties. There is no standard way of handling tenant-required improvements to a commercial property.

Are commercial leases generally for 12 months like residential leases?

Like everything else about commercial leases, there is not a set term for which they are written. They can range from month-to-month to 99 years. One big difference between a commercial lease and a residential lease is the fact that a Lessee can be held liable for the remaining term of a commercial lease even if he or she decides to vacate the property years before the lease expires.

What is a "build to suit commercial lease," and how does it work?

A "build to suit lease" refers to a lease in which the Lessor agrees to build a specific type of building to suit the tenant's needs. An example of this would be a trademark design building such as one for Pizza Hut, McDonald's, or any other franchised business that has to have a particular design. When this type lease is entered into, the Lessor generally charges a lease rate adequate to pay for the cost of the building plus a profit during the initial term of the lease. If the Lessor is borrowing money to construct the building, the lender will rely substantially on the tenant's creditworthiness and ability to pay. When a Lessee enters into a lease such as this, it is understood that he or she will be responsible for making the lease payments even if the business closes.

31

Building Your Support Team

The sooner you build a support team of people who will help you to move quickly when the time comes, the sooner you will be able to truly call yourself a real estate investor. Having lawyers, accountants, bankers, real estate agents, management personnel, subcontractors, and other such people you can call on for quick action can mean the difference between making a deal and losing it.

Having good relations with real estate agents, bankers, attorneys, and title companies is critical to having the ability to close quickly when you have a chance to make a wholesale purchase. Often you get the opportunity to make a good buy just because you're able to close quickly.

Building relations with subcontractors that will drop what they're doing to jump on a project for you is also important. As we were writing the final chapters of this book, Mike leased a 12,000-square-foot building he owned to a school. The interior of the building was largely unfinished and had to be completely up-fitted to accommodate the tenant. The challenge was that the lease was signed on June 30, and the tenant had to be in the building before August 1. That left only one month to complete finishing the sheetrock, plumbing, electrical, doors and trim, painting, and the construction of a parking lot to accommodate over 80 cars. The tenant was in by the third week in July.

The relationships Mike has built over the years enabled him to call the various subcontractors he needed to do the work, and they all dropped what they were doing to expedite getting Mike's building ready in record time. The best way to build this kind of relationship with building contractors is to establish a reputation for prompt payment when the work is completed. The people who work for Mike know that when they present him with an invoice, they usually will receive payment within 24 to 48 hours.

Let's now look at some of the questions readers have asked us about building these kinds of relationships with a support team.

I'm working on building better banking relations, and I know that this starts with improving my credit and my FICO score. The problem I have is that I'm going on three trips next year, and it will be difficult to obtain financing because I'm spending so much on the trips. What do you think about me flipping a house or two to get some working capital before I start keeping properties the Weekend Millionaire way?

Our question to you is, "Are the trips as important to you in the long run as a couple of properties could be?" The sights you want to see on these trips probably still will be there long after you get established and have the income to support going on such trips. Struggling to go now may put you even further behind the eight ball, and it could be years, if ever, before you get established financially. Weigh the costs against the benefits of both, and you will make the right decision.

Do you have problems with lenders as far as the number of loans you can get from them?

All banks have lending limits. Small banks can have very small limits . . . $500,000 or less. Even if their limits are small, banks can bring in other participating banks if they like the deal enough. With this said, all banks have comfort levels based on the experience, net worth, and cash flow of the borrower. This comfort level is reached most often before the lending limit. For this reason, we feel that it is better to spread your business around and cultivate relationships with numerous banks.

Some of the lenders tell me that they can only do so many loans. How do you buy many, many properties if you can only get a limited number of loans from your lenders?

What your banker may be telling you is that once you reach a certain number of loans, you are no longer considered a passive investor, and your loans cannot be sold on the secondary market. If your bank does not want to keep the loans in its portfolio, it is going to limit the number of them it makes. This may be what you are running up against.

If that is the case, what kind of strategy should I consider?

You need to build relationships with several banks. Each one may hold a certain number of loans in its own portfolio. Another reason for cultivating relationships with many banks is so that you don't have to ride the ups and downs of a single bank. For example, Mike once had 29 loans with one bank that all had five-year balloons. Following the bank's merger with another bank that was awash in bad real estate loans, the new bank refused to renew any of his loans when they came due, even though he was never late with a payment and had substantial cash deposits in the bank. This is how he learned not to put all his eggs in one basket . . . or in this case one bank.

Rather than cultivating some other real estate agent, how do you feel about becoming a licensed agent yourself in order to have access to the Multiple Listing Service (MLS)?

Mike and Roger disagree on this question. Roger thinks that having a license is an asset, but Mike feels that it is a negative for investors. Yes, being a licensed agent does give you access to the MLS (if you subscribe to the service) and other good information, as Roger suggests, but Mike feels that the added scrutiny and disclosure requirements that come with a license make it more of a liability than an asset for an investor. On this question, you'll have to make you own decision based on your personal comfort level.

Moving into Larger Properties

How do I find a good real estate agent who will give me his or her number and work with me!

The best way to build a relationship with a broker or agent is to find one whom you like and then use him or her for all your deals. If you find a property listed with another broker, call the one you work with and let him or her present your offer. Real estate commissions usually are split between the selling agent and the listing agent. If you allow your agent to participate in the selling-agent commission on a few deals, the incentive is much greater for him or her to bring you any deals he or she lists or other deals he or she learns about through the MLS or other sources. It's the old "you scratch my back and I'll scratch yours" theory.

Do you recommend using a buyer's broker?

We absolutely recommend a buyer's broker. Not for every deal, but having one who will work with you gives you several options. A good buyer's broker is an essential part of a strong support team. The more you work with a buyer's broker and the better understanding he or she has of your goals, the more he or she can help you.

Do you recommend joining a real estate investment club as a way to find members of your support team?

This is a difficult question to answer without offending someone. Real estate clubs are great for gathering information, plus you get to hang around people who are active in real estate investing, but we're not sure how many members of a strong support team you will find there. Our experience is that you cultivate and build your support team; you don't go out and find it at a club meeting.

What can I expect to gain from a real estate investment club?

Real estate clubs will bring in speakers (such as Mike Summey), but the best part is hanging around with investors who know the local market and will give you encouragement. Just the level of excitement that is generated by a room full of real estate investors is often worth the price of admission . . .

which is usually very low in relation to what you get for the money. We recommend real estate investment clubs for all new investors.

When you speak of tax advisors, are you using a tax advisor who focuses on real estate transactions, or is an H&R Block representative adequate?

We recommend that you use a CPA who is familiar with the tax code. While some H&R Block representatives may be fine, they do not have the training that a CPA is required to have. Tax advisors are like many other things; some are better than others. We recommend that you interview several before deciding on one.

What services should I expect from a CPA?

The most important thing you should expect from your CPA is advice. Sure, most CPA firms have bookkeepers who can handle your accounting if you need it, but in most cases the CPA will advise you on tax matters and estate planning and oversee the preparation of your tax returns. A good CPA also can help you to analyze proposed purchases or at least review your analysis and increase your comfort level when making offers.

Should I use a real estate attorney, or is a title company adequate when buying?

Different states do things differently. In North Carolina, where Mike lives, real estate closings generally are handled by real estate attorneys. In southern California, where Roger resides, escrow companies handle most closings. In northern California, it's real estate attorneys. What's most important, regardless of where you live, is that you get an insured title when you buy.

I find that many bankers add what I call bogus fees to deals. How do you find one who understands your goals and doesn't try to stick it to you on every deal?

Loan officers often make commissions based on the rates and fees they are able to negotiate on loans. Sometimes you have to train them and help them to understand that they don't make anything on the loans that don't close. You strengthen your negotiating position when you have more than one option.

I'm planning to take a banker friend to lunch to start establishing a professional relationship. Should I identify a property to talk about first?

Not necessarily. A good conversation over lunch can help you to understand your banker and allow him or her to get to know you better. Trust is the biggest factor in building banking relations. If you outline your goals and how you plan to achieve them, when you do find a property that fits within those guidelines, your banker knows that you are serious and are following a plan, not just making a knee-jerk reaction.

How much information should I share with my banker? I always thought that the less a banker knows, the better it is for me.

Mike provides all his banks with a monthly statement showing each property, what it brings in for the month, what expenses are paid for it during the month, and the overall totals for all properties showing total income, expenses, profit, depreciation, and cash flow. He does this every month by the tenth of the month, and his bankers all love him for it. When bank examiners come, they hope his file is one of the ones they look at. We don't recommend withholding information because it only breeds mistrust and creates doubt.

My banker said that he wouldn't make me a loan if I dealt with another bank. What should I do in this situation?

Find another banker!

When do you use an agent to represent you when buying, and when do you do it on your own?

We nearly always use an agent. We find that it frees us up to look for more properties, and we don't have to worry about all the details that are required to close transactions. We feel that real estate agents earn what they're paid, if for no other reason, because they can facilitate easier closings.

Should I write my own offers and then have a real estate agent present them to the sellers?

Building Your Support Team

It all depends on how experienced you are with making offers; in the beginning, a good buyer's broker can assist you greatly in drafting offers. As a professional, the buyer's broker should know all the things that should be included in your offers and can advise you accordingly. Just be sure that you don't allow him or her to influence you in what you want to offer. Remember that you are the one who will have to pay for the property once you own it.

I figure that the more brokers I work with, the more people I will have helping me to find good rental properties. Do you agree with this philosophy, or should I work with just one broker exclusively?

Each situation is different. Much depends on how strong your relationship is with the broker. Mike primarily uses just one broker who represents him, but he works with dozens of other brokers to find properties. It takes a long time to build the kind of relationship Mike has cultivated. In the beginning, he worked with many different brokers until he found one he wanted to work with exclusively. Now he runs nearly all his transactions through this one broker. Do what feels comfortable to you and what seems to get you the best results.

If you have a broker representing you when buying, when would you need to use the negotiating skills you teach in The Weekend Millionaire's Secrets to Investing in Real Estate?

We would challenge the broker to get the offer accepted but reserve the right to meet with the seller if the broker can't do it. This really challenges brokers to go for it, but on occasion we do have to meet face to face with sellers to learn their needs and to structure offers that work for them as well as us.

In creating your team, how important is it to find a good maintenance person? Do you do this, or is that something you can have your property manager do for you?

For general maintenance work, we let the management companies find the maintenance people. This is part of the service they provide, and if we choose the people they have to work with, it gives them an excuse when they don't perform up to our standards. For major repairs or improvements, we like to use our own subcontractors who answer directly to us. We seldom give our management companies authority to make major repairs because we want to know what we are getting and be sure that the work is done by people we trust and know we can go back to if there are any problems.

The agent I am currently using is experienced, but he continually knocks my offers. He seems to want to be in charge and tell me what I should do, and as a result, I find myself constantly fighting with him over my offers. What should I do in this situation?

Find an agent who understands investors and wants to work with them. If an agent balks at presenting the offer you want to make, this is the first sign that you should get another agent. Agents are obligated to present every offer, regardless what they think of it, but if they aren't enthusiastic about the offers, they won't do much of a job when they present them. If they are working for you as a buyer's agent, remind them that they are obliged to not only present the offer but also to advocate your position. It is their job, and they could lose their license by not doing so, but be realistic, if they don't believe in the offer, they aren't going to be much of an advocate.

I am in the process of assembling my support team, and I have a fraternity brother who owns his own mortgage company. He essentially closes deals and immediately sells them in the secondary market. Am I better off establishing a relationship directly with a bank in order to get the best deals, or does it make sense to have an intermediary?

A lot depends on your credit and financial position. If your credit is marginal and you don't have a lot of cash, you may have little choice but to work with a mortgage broker. If you have excellent credit and cash reserves, you may be able to do as well by going directly to the banks, but keep in mind that mortgage brokers often have access to many more sources than you can find yourself. Although mortgage brokers are middlemen and have to make a profit too . . . they often can beat the deals the banks offer. The key is to find an honest and reputable mortgage broker who will accept a reasonable profit and won't try to pad deals with excess fees. Your fraternity brother may fit this mold.

Building Your Support Team

Would you consider builders to be a part of your support team? I'm meeting with a builder to discuss buying a few of his houses and want to get a good deal.

There may be some situations where a builder could be considered part of a support team, but we would rather think of builders as a potential source of good properties. Mike made a local builder an offer to take several units at a deep discount if they remained unsold by the time they were completed. Under this arrangement, the builder could go ahead and start construction on several units at once and list them for sale at preconstruction retail prices. The builder knows that he can keep building because he can turn any unsold units at wholesale prices if they don't sell during construction. This security allows him to keep building out the development and keep his crews working even if a few units don't sell quickly.

I didn't see any references to credit issues in The Weekend Millionaire's Secrets to Investing in Real Estate *or on your Web site. Why is this? Since getting loans is based heavily on credit scores, how do the different credit ratings factor into being a successful investor? Should one assume that if your credit isn't perfect, you can forget about becoming a real estate investor?*

Naturally, if you have some cash and good credit, things are easier, but the lack of one or both of these is no reason to assume that you can't be successful. When Mike started, he had very little money and marginal credit. This meant that he had to look a little harder to find deals. Initially, you probably will have to locate properties in which the owners owe very little or nothing so that you can deal directly with them on financing. It is up to you to sell yourself as a responsible person and a good risk in order to get them to agree to owner financing. You also can obtain low debt-to-equity first-mortgage loans from individual investors (e.g., a loan for 20 to 40 percent of appraisal) and combine this with owner financing for the balance. These deals are more difficult to find, but they aren't impossible. This added difficulty is the price everyone must pay for lack of cash and credit. We suggest that you read and study Chapter 31 of the book, particularly the part about building banking relations. It tells you what you need to learn and do to establish the good credit you need to get loans from banks. Don't get discouraged if things don't happen overnight. It took Mike years to build a good, solid credit rating. As explained in the book, building good credit takes time, and as an investor, you need to go through at least one full boom and bust cycle of the real estate economy to demonstrate that you can make it through the bad times as well as the good.

If you could recommend one thing that you feel is most important to building relationships with your support team, what would it be?

No doubt it would be to reward the members of your support team at every opportunity you get. People are more inclined to put you at the top of their "to do" list when they know that you will recommend them to others. The brokers, attorneys, accountants, bankers, contractors, and other members of your support team are trying to build their businesses too. Whenever one of them does a good job for you, brag about him or her to everyone you know. Don't miss an opportunity to recommend members of your support team to friends and acquaintances that you know would make good clients. By the same token, don't send them a bunch of deadbeats who can only waste their time. A good support team is there to propel you forward, not to prop you up. The same is true for the people you recommend.

PART VII

Getting Started

In this part of *The Weekend Millionaire's Secrets to Investing in Real Estate,* Chapters 32 through 39 outline exercises to be done during the first eight weeks of your investing career. These chapters are very self-explanatory and have produced few questions; therefore, we will not attempt to answer questions about them. In Chapter 32 of this book we will address questions from Chapter 40 of the book, "The 14 Biggest Mistakes New Investors Make."

We could easily have lumped many of the questions we have already answered into this part, but we tried to put as many of them as possible into sections to which they were more directly related. It is only natural for new investors to become exuberant when they experience success and want to repeat this feeling as quickly as possible. For others yet to experience success, seeing others make purchases often gives them a feeling of being left behind, which causes them to make many of the mistakes mentioned in the final chapter.

Between the mistakes of "being impatient" and "procrastinating," two things that each of us can control, lay a variety of other mistakes that stem from lack of knowledge. In our book *Weekend Millionaire Mindset: How Ordinary People Can Achieve Extraordinary Success* we describe those with the characteristics of procrastinating and being impatient as "tortoises" and "hares" and explain why both become road kill on life's economic highway. We strongly recommend that you read this book if you're serious about wanting to build wealth. We also recommend that you encourage your children to read it before they enter the workplace. As our friend Carleton Sheets says in the foreword to the book, ". . . it should be required reading for every high school student in America and most of the adults too."

As we come to the end of this book, we want our readers to understand that we truly believe that ordinary working people can achieve financial independence if they will just commit themselves to some commonsense principles and understand that building wealth doesn't happen overnight. The biggest reason we are writing the *Weekend Millionaire* series of books is that we believe that the greatest disservice successful people can do to their fellow humans is to go to their grave and take with them the knowledge that helped them achieve their success. These books and our award-winning Web site weekendmillionaire.com (which you will learn more about in the following Bonus Section) are our way of giving back some of what we've learned on our journey to financial independence.

The following questions address some of the mistakes that many new investors could avoid with a little common sense and improved knowledge . . . knowledge we hope they will gain by reading our books.

32

The 14 Biggest Mistakes New Investors Make

As we come to the end of this book, we want you to know that we have truly enjoyed sharing our knowledge of long-term real estate investing and have especially enjoyed participating with our readers in the live online chats we host on our Web site. Many of the questions contained in this book originated in one of those chats. Over the months since *The Weekend Millionaire's Secrets to Investing in Real Estate* was released, we have received thousands of questions. In this book we have consolidated and grouped these questions into chapters that correspond directly with the chapters in *The Weekend Millionaire's Secrets to Investing in Real Estate* and have provided more detailed answers than is possible in the chats. This has resulted in a companion tool that goes hand in hand with our real estate book.

In the Bonus Section that follows, our Web master, Ralph Roberts, takes you on a tour of our Web site weekendmillionaire.com and gives you insight into how to get the most from it. The site is a continuously evolving Web site that changes daily. We hope that you will take the time to read and study the Bonus Section and become a regular user of the Web site.

Now let's move on to answer some of the questions we have received about the 14 biggest mistakes new investors make.

Why do you recommend setting up separate bank accounts in which to deposit the income and pay the bills from your investment properties?

We recommend that you set up a separate bank account to handle your rental income and expenses and treat it as you would a retirement account. Investing for long-term wealth building the Weekend Millionaire way is much easier and less tempting when you segregate the funds from your investment properties and then let them build up separately from your earned income until you accumulate enough to have comfortable cash reserves and to make other purchases. Unless you separate your funds, the temptation to spend them on nonessential items becomes so great that the money can slip away easily. Remember, the goal of becoming a Weekend Millionaire is to reach the point where the income from your investments is enough to maintain your standard of living for the rest of your life. Only then can you say that you are totally financially independent.

What's the real reason that you say buying high-end or low-end properties is a mistake?

There are no hidden reasons for staying away from these properties. We cover the real reasons fairly well in *The Weekend Millionaire's Secrets to Investing in Real Estate.* You always will be able to find what seem to be great deals in both expensive and inexpensive properties, but these don't make good long-term rental investments. You may be able to find some high-end properties that you can buy for 50 percent of appraised value, but even at that price, you still may have to rent them for three, four, or five times the average rent "bread and butter" properties are bringing. These properties are much harder to rent, and they stay vacant much longer between tenants. At the other end of the scale, properties that can be bought very cheaply are often in bad neighborhoods where the qualities of the tenants they attract are less than desirable. You always can find renters for low-end properties, but repair costs tend to be very high and collections difficult. These are just some of the reasons why you're better off to stick with properties in the midrange of the rental market for your area.

The 14 Biggest Mistakes New Investors Make

When I prepare a financial statement for the bank, do I list my properties at what I paid for them or what I think they are worth?

You certainly can list your properties based on their fair market value, but whatever value you list, you should be able to support it if your banker questions it. Nothing will destroy your credibility with lenders faster that puffing up your financial statements with unrealistic values on your properties. The method Mike currently uses is to show the value of his properties at actual cost, tax value, or latest certified appraised value, whichever is higher, and then add 3 percent annually to adjust for inflation. He varies this amount based on market conditions but always uses a percentage that is 1 to 3 percent below the actual amount properties are appreciating. The only time he deviates from this amount is when properties are reassessed for tax purposes or when a new certified appraisal is obtained, at which time he will adjust the base value and start the estimated annual appreciation over based on the new amount.

I know that you say that it is not good to try to make repairs yourself, but I can't find properties to buy that will rent for enough to pay management and repair costs and leave anything left over for me. What's wrong with doing the work myself and saving the money? Am I not, in effect, earning whatever I save because I don't have to pay that out to someone else?

If you like to do that kind of work and have the time to do it, there's nothing wrong with it. When it becomes a mistake is when you find yourself painting, patching leaks, and unclogging toilets rather than looking for additional properties to buy. Let's assume that you spend four hours a week doing repair work that you would have to pay someone else $25 per hour to do. In a year you would save about $5,000 in labor. Not bad, you say! But assume that you spent the same four hours a week looking at properties and making offers, and you only bought one property during the entire year; it's very possible that one property will earn you more per year for the rest of your life than what you saved, which is only a savings for that one year. Assume that you could save this amount of money each year doing repairs. In 10 years, you would realize a savings of $50,000 to $100,000. This may seem like a lot of money if you're currently working a $30,000 a year job, but let's look at it a little differently. Assume that you spent this time inspecting properties and making offers, and as a result, you bought just one property per year. Let's also assume that between debt reduction, appreciation, and cash flow, the combination of equity growth and cash flow is $5,000 to $10,000 per year per property. The second year you would be realizing a gain of $10,000 to $20,000, the third year this would grow to $15,000 to $30,000, and by the tenth year this annual amount with 10 properties would be between $50,000 and $100,000, or exactly as much per year as what you might save in 10 years of doing your own repairs. Does it make sense now? We want you to look at the big picture and use your time doing the things that will contribute most to making you rich.

My parents once owned a rental house, and it seemed like every time they rented it, the tenants trashed the place. How can I just forget my dad's words, "Son, don't ever become a landlord," and feel comfortable about investing the way you advocate?

Your parents may have had a bad experience, but all you have to do is to look at all the people who have created huge fortunes in real estate to know that your parents' experience is the exception, not the rule. It sounds like they are a typical example of why we recommend using professional property managers. Most individuals rent to people based on their gut feel about them. Professional managers pull credit reports and criminal histories on people before they will rent to them. These reports often reveal patterns of behavior that send up red flags that make renting to them a risky proposition. People with this kind of history often prey on individuals like your parents who may not check their backgrounds because they know it will be extremely difficult to find a professional manager who will rent to them. These types of people become very good at coming across great in an interview but revert to their old selves once they move in.

I live in San Francisco, and I can tell you that there is no way to find properties within 10 miles of where I live that can be rented for enough to justify the prices property is selling for here. Should I just give up on trying to buy the way you recommend, or should I try to invest elsewhere?

This is an area that we should have expanded on in *The Weekend Millionaire's Secrets to Investing in Real Estate.* Our suggestion of buying within a 10-mile radius of where you live works about 80 to 90 percent of the time; however, we failed to address the fact that it is very difficult to make our formulas work in close proximity to some major cities. Our intent in suggesting the 10-mile radius of where you live was to encourage you to keep your investments grouped into an area small enough to allow you to ride by them on a regular basis. If you are in one of the major cities where this is difficult to do, our suggestion is to look far enough away to where you can find properties for which you can make the numbers work and then concentrate your efforts in a 10-mile radius from that point. What we don't want to see you do is have investment properties so scattered that you can't give adequate attention to them. You may have good managers in scattered places, but never forget the fact that managers, like most other contractors, are more inclined to do what you inspect, not what you expect.

We got a free two-night stay in exchange for sitting through a two-hour presentation and taking a tour of the grounds of a beachfront condo project in Florida that is under construction. They showed us how the units will cash flow if they are only rented half the year. Since we've returned home, they've called us five times to try to get us to buy one of the units. Wouldn't this be a good first investment, especially since they will take care of all the management and maintenance?

If these units are such good investments, they wouldn't be giving away free vacation packages and calling you repeatedly to get you to buy. If they are truly good investments, investors would be snatching them up as fast as they could be built. What you experienced is the typical sales pitch many developers use to sell this type of project. They are excellent at creating so much hype that unsuspecting buyers get caught in the euphoria of what seems to be a no-lose proposition. We don't recommend this type of property as an investment. If you want a beachfront condo for your own use and need it to produce some income in order to afford it, a project such as this might be worth looking into, but don't think of it as an investment.

We all know that property values and rents have been going up steadily for years. Wouldn't it be okay to buy properties that have some negative cash flow knowing that it won't be long before the rents can be raised?

Getting Started

While you may be in a financial position that would allow you to make up the shortfall on properties that won't generate cash flow, why would you want to do this? Why would you want to take part of your earned income and use it to support properties that are supposed to be adding to your income? Entering into purchases that won't generate cash flow is often the result of being impatient. You make several offers that are rejected, and each one convinces you a little more that you will have to accept negative cash flows if you are going to buy anything. We recommend that you stay the course and keep making offers that work with the net operating income (NOI). Don't bet on rents going up to bail you out. If they do go up, it's a bonus, but if they don't, you're still okay when you insist on at least a breakeven cash flow from the beginning.

I am a graduating college student at Penn State University. I read The Weekend Millionaire's Secrets to Investing in Real Estate, *along with several other books, and am looking to get into investment real estate. I feel like I can relate to you because when you started, you were around 20 years old and really didn't have much money. I am graduating this spring and have virtually no money. From your book, I don't know how I can even start your program. For instance, once I find a house I want to invest in, how do I get financing? Can I just go into a bank and ask for a loan? Also, how do I rent a single-family home? Don't most people like to own a home? Why would I want to rent? Don't most neighborhoods frown on renting? Wouldn't it be better to look for houses in a tourist area? I have studied the art of negotiating and really want to do this. I have so many questions, but I am young and eager to learn. Can you help me?*

You pose some very interesting questions that we think most young people have when facing life in the real world. Mike has two sons who hit him with some of the same questions. One is 23 and has graduated recently from Florida State University, and the other is 21 and is currently a senior at Furman University in South Carolina. The advice he gave them is to read the book over and over and study the concepts contained in it. Everything you need to know is in the book, plus a lot of things that are probably out of your reach until you become more established financially. Naturally, if you have some cash and good credit, you have more options than someone who doesn't. Your first order of business when you graduate should be to put your financial house in order before you start trying to buy real estate. If you have credit card debt or student loans, get them paid off as quickly as possible. Consumer debt will hurt you more than anything when you get ready to start investing. In the beginning it will be much more difficult to find properties because you don't have cash to put down or good enough credit to get financing from banks. During this time, you need to keep making offers that will work for you and that you will be able to handle when one is accepted. These probably will involve asking the seller to provide the financing and hold the property as security. You may even have to make offers to lease the property with an option to buy at a later date and ask for all or part of the rent you pay to be applied to the purchase price. If an offer such as this is accepted, you could then live in the property and pay the rent while you build up equity or sublease the property to someone else for more than the rent you have to pay. Don't worry about people not wanting to rent . . . there are plenty of people who have no other choice. Just be careful what kind of properties you buy . . . and most important, study the last chapter of the book very carefully.

I've read The Weekend Millionaire's Secrets to Investing in Real Estate, *I've studied your audio program, I've read probably a dozen other books and listened to numerous audio and video programs on real estate investing, but I just can't seem to get started. I've written at least 50 offers but have never gotten up the courage to present one of them. How do I get beyond this hangup and actually buy something?*

It sounds like you may be suffering from the "paralysis of analysis" syndrome. We've had many questions similar to yours, and they all seem to be asking the same thing, "What can I do to develop the mindset required to become an investor?" We left this question until last because it addresses a problem that we wrote an entire book to answer. Our best-selling book, *Weekend Millionaire Mindset: How Ordinary People Can Achieve Extraordinary Success,* takes you through a journey from the Formative Years to the Learning Years and the Earning Years. In it we address the obstacles, impediments, barriers, difficulties, road blocks, snags, and other problems that everyone faces in life and show you how to go over, under, around, or through them to achieve the things you want in life. The final three chapters of that book are "Creating Desire," "Eliminating Excuses," and "Getting Started." We strongly urge everyone who has read our real estate book and is now reading this book to get a copy of *Weekend Millionaire Mindset* and study it carefully. Not only will it answer the preceding question, but it also will help you in virtually any endeavor you undertake.

Finally, if you haven't found the answer to your question in this book, we have another great resource for you. Our Web site weekendmillionaire.com is great place to get more information and to talk directly with Mike and Roger. They host *free* online chats for their readers and any others who have questions. These chats are live and often include guests on a variety of subjects ranging from real estate investing to finance, asset protection, insurance, negotiating, and more. If you will visit the Web site and register as a "New User," you will receive e-mail notices about the dates and times of the chats and additional information on any guests that may be in the chats.

The following Bonus Section is written by our Web master, Ralph Roberts, and it will take you on a tour of weekendmillionaire.com and explain how to get the most from it and show you how it can become a tremendous resource for improving your future.

Bonus Section

Getting Real Estate Information 24/7

This section introduces you to our Web site weekendmillionaire.com. These days most authors have Web sites, but those sites usually resemble nothing more than a brochure advertising their books. Our site—weekendmillionaire.com (it works equally well with or without the *www* in front)—goes far beyond being a mere electronic advertising handout.

Weekendmillionaire.com interacts with you, responding and generating pages "on the fly" and matching the choices you make by clicking on various buttons and other links. Sites with these advanced features are called "dynamic" Web sites. Using an underlying database, weekendmillionaire.com currently has the capacity to generate many thousands of pages, all in a simple, easy-to-understand manner, for those of us who just want to learn real estate investing and not computer programming.

The four chapters that follow show you the basics of the site:

- *Touring the Web site.* First, you'll see ways to find the Web site and understand its layout. We introduce you to navigation, menus, searching the entire site, and other ways to find what *you* want to find. Then we give you a tour, showing you where everything is located and how each item works, with pictures included.

- *Chats.* Next comes a chapter all about our online *chats*. Our weekly formal chats are easily one of our most popular features. In fact, these chats helped to created this book, since many of the questions answered in these pages were first asked us during chats. In the chapter about chats, we talk you through the simple methods of connecting to and using the chat software and how to find out when chats will be occurring. Join us online and get *your* questions answered in real time!
- *Forums.* Our *forums* section describes how our online bulletin board works. Find the answers to hundreds of questions here, and post questions of your own. The forums are always available to you 24/7.
- *Other.* Finally, we show you how to find our site more easily and how to find literally *tons* of other real estate and wealth-building sites. We also give you useful contacts for getting additional assistance on investing fundamentals and for any questions that may come up on how the Web site works.

We don't abandon you after you walk out of the store with our books because weekendmillionaire.com will give you ongoing support, enlightenment, encouragement, inspiration, and yep, even entertainment for years to come.

Enjoy, and please visit us often at weekendmillionaire.com. We're as near as your computer!

B1

Touring the Web Site

The official Weekend Millionaire Web site (weekendmillionaire.com) generated much of this book. Users of the Web site, our wonderful participants in the weekly *chats* (typing back and forth to each other in real time), readers who posted on the forums (our electronic bulletin boards), and folks who e-mailed us asked the questions we answered in these pages.

Think of our Web site as exactly what it is, an easy-to-use enhancement to the books, audio programs, and personal events presented by Mike Summey and Roger Dawson—an enhancement available 24/7, any time of the day or night you find convenient. You'll discover that the site becomes an important part of your profitable growth in using the Weekend Millionaire concepts for real estate investing and developing a general mindset for success in life. And this site is totally free!

This Bonus Section shows you how the Web site works. It consists of four chapters—a generalized tour of the Web site (this chapter), how the chat works, how the forum works, and a final chapter about some other ways to obtain information using our system and the Internet.

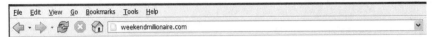

Figure B1-1 Just type weekendmillionaire.com in the address line window (shown here using *Firefox*).

Finding the Web Site

We're on a computer near you. The Weekend Millionaire Web site works with all major Web *browsers* (software used in viewing Web pages). Chances are you have one of the "biggies," such as *Internet Explorer,* Mozilla's *Firefox, Opera,* or (if yours is an Apple Macintosh computer) perhaps *Safari.*

All the browsers so far mentioned, and most others, have a small address window at the top where you type in the Web address of the site you want to view. For our site, simply type

weekendmillionaire.com

Back in the early nineties—when the Web was a brand-new protocol on the Internet—such additions as *http://* (for Hypertext Transfer Protocol) and *www* (World Wide Web) were necessary parts of Web addresses, or Uniform Resource Locators (URLs). Today, why would you want to remember and use all that technical stuff? It's not necessary. We've programmed the site so that weekendmillionaire.com is the only address needed (as shown in Figure B1-1).

How It Works

All Web sites on the World Wide Web fall into one of two categories—*static* or *dynamic*. Here's an analogy showing the difference. Someone hands you an 8.5 × 11 inch sheet of paper that's a flyer. It's for a yard sale a family down the street is having. You tape it on your wall. No matter how much you stare at that piece of paper, it never changes. It just gives you the same message over and over. Someone may come in one day and cross out "Starts at 8 a.m." and put "Starts at 8:30 a.m."—but not often.

This gets pretty darn dull after you've read the flyer on your wall a few times. It's static, and the word "static" means "unchanging"—also "boring." Not to mention "uninformative."

Touring the Web Site

Now contrast that to hanging one of those spiffy new flat-screen high-definition televisions on that same wall (take down the tacky flyer first; you've got it memorized by now). Hook it up to cable or a dish antenna. Click the remote. Now you've got hundreds of channels at your instant beck and call. That's "dynamic"! You can find useful and entertaining information now.

Our site—weekendmillionaire.com (see Figure B1-2 for the main or "Home" page)—is a "dynamic" site. It uses a mix of various programming languages (primarily PHP and Python) to access databases (both MySQL and PostgreSQL) depending on what information you request. In simple terms,

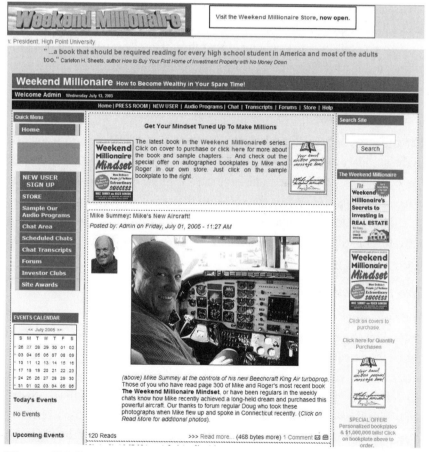

Figure B1-2 The main page of weekendmillionaire.com serves as your starting point in using the site.

the site "interacts" with you and builds Web pages on the fly that supply whatever information you request. Currently, this system constructs many thousands of discrete pages and has the capacity for many more. You'll never get bored, bubba!

Technical Requirements

We've designed the site so that all you do is point and click on various topic choices depending on your interest of the moment. To operate weekend-millionaire.com and access its many thousands of pages, all you need to do is move the mouse cursor and tap the left mouse button (and if you have gotten as far as *any* Web site, you probably know how to do this). As the cliché goes, "It ain't rocket science."

Our goal, always, is simplicity of operation. The site exists to make it easy to find and learn real estate investing techniques and ways of honing your mindset so that you employ these techniques efficiently and successfully.

Flash and Java

The site's two only really technical requirements for best usage are covered in the standard configurations of most browsers—*Flash* and *Java*. We use *Flash* in serving video and audio programs (Figure B1-3 shows some of our video selections). *Java* runs the software that enables weekly chats.

Should video and audio not work for you, or the chat program does not activate, consult the "Help" feature in your browser software for activating *Flash* or *Java*, respectively.

The Need for Speed

The only other note about technical requirements concerns *speed*. Speed is good on the information highway—the more speed, the better. Dial-up connections continue their slide into obsolescence. More and more sites require DSL, cable, or some other form of high-speed connection. Our site—weekendmillionaire.com—still works fine on dial-up (albeit slower, eh?), with the exception of video and audio. Rich media (the buzz term for video and so forth) requires *bandwidth* (receiving more data in a shorter time). So get cable or DSL for the fullest Internet experience.

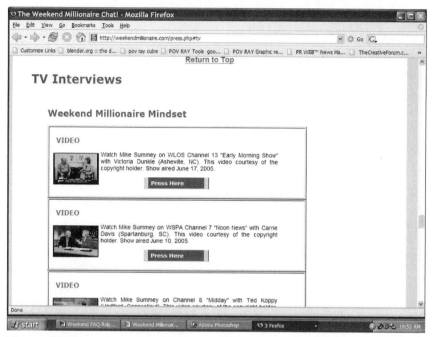

Figure B1-3 *Flash* video lets you watch interviews of Mike and Roger at your convenience.

Getting Around

Besides being dynamic, weekendmillionaire.com is also an *evolving* Web site—which just means we're continually adding features and information. So this and the next three chapters show the site as it is at this moment, and by the time this book gets published, you'll see a good deal more. But the basics described here will still apply, and the site itself will help you to get around and find things.

Menus

Collections of "links" (buttons or underlined text) on a Web page are called "menus." Clicking on a menu item (link) is the primary way you navigate on any Web page. The click causes the view in your browser to change to another page or perhaps to a different place on the same page.

Getting Real Estate Information 24/7

As an example, the menu "bar" appears near the top of most pages (see Figure B1-4). The links in this area are shortcuts to nine of the most often used areas of the site. We'll be adding more later. Fuller descriptions appear later, but these links are

Home—Takes you back to the main or "Home" page, which is your starting page.

PRESS ROOM—This is an extensive area designed for the working press, but everyone's welcome to explore it. Numerous radio and TV interviews (with streaming video and sound) may be listened to or viewed. And if you are a member of the media, you can find press releases and/or a handy form to schedule interviews with Mike or Roger (click on the "Request Interview" button).

NEW USER—Opens the sign-up page to become a member of the weekendmillionaire.com site. Membership is free and gives you access to additional features anonymous surfers cannot use, such as the ability to post in the forums. Join us—there are a growing number of other privileges only available to registered members of the site. See the "Signing Up" section below for more information on registering.

Audio Programs—A sampling of (listen to actual excerpts) and information about the audio and video programs on real estate investment and power negotiating published by Mike Summey and Roger Dawson.

Chat—The online chats remain one of our most popular events. Chapter B2 shows you how chats work.

Transcripts—We record transcripts of our weekly formal chats (this is what generated many of the questions we answered in this book!). This area lets you read these transcripts going back to our first chat on November 21, 2003.

Weekend Millionaire How to Become Wealthy in Your Spare Time!
Welcome ralph Thursday July 14, 2005
Home | PRESS ROOM | NEW USER | Audio Programs | Chat | Transcripts | Forums | Store | Help

Figure B1-4 One of our menus is usually at the top of the current page.

Forums—The forums are our electronic bulletin boards on topics related to the themes of weekendmillionaire.com. We feel that this area is important enough to warrant a chapter of its own (see Chapter B3).

Store—The store is just that, a secure shopping area where you can order extra copies of this or the other books in the *Weekend Millionaire* series, audio and video programs, and specialty items such as autographed bookplates not available elsewhere.

Help—The help area is, like the four chapters in this Bonus Section, another way to find out how the site works and how you can get the most benefit and enjoyment from it.

More links and menus (groups of links and buttons) exist and help you to navigate around this extensive Web site. We'll show you more of these during the grand tour of the site in the latter part of this chapter.

Searches

Menus and links fill your need *if* you know where you're going, right? But on a Web site that generates many *thousands* of pages, how do you find stuff when you have no idea where it hides?

"Seek, and ye shall find," it says in the Good Book. This applies to the weekendmillionaire.com site also. Use the "Search" feature, and much will be revealed unto you. Look in the right-hand column of the "Home" page for the "Search Site" box (see Figure B1-5).

Try this feature out. Type a word into the box and see how many times it appears on the site. You'll see a list of the articles or other areas that have this word, and when you click on the link generated (it will be green), the site transports you to the appropriate page.

Figure B1-5 Typing a word or phrase in the "Search Site" box finds all references to that term on the site.

Signing Up

Membership does have its advantages. It's free and gives you access to additional features anonymous surfers cannot use, such as the ability to post in the forums. Also, you can send private messages to other users, receive e-mails of upcoming events, and get our newsletter, all at no charge.

Registering

The easiest way to join is by clicking the "New User" button on the black menu bar near the top of our site. This gives you the sign-up page shown in Figure B1-6.

Joining the site is reasonably straightforward. In the form shown in Figure B1-6, choose a user name. This name can be anything you like *but should not contain any spaces.* Use an underscore character (_) for spaces if you want a name like Roger_Dawson (and who wouldn't?). If the name is already taken, the system tells you and allows you to choose another name (user names must be unique).

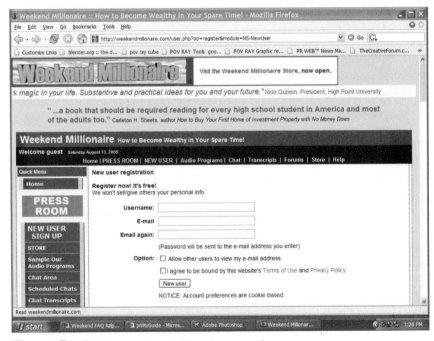

Figure B1-6 The weekendmillionaire.com sign-up page.

Enter your e-mail address next, and then enter it again in the "E-mail again" box. This procedure is very important because it verifies your e-mail. The password for the site will be sent to the e-mail address specified.

Click in the "Option" box whether or not you want others to see your e-mail address. We suggest that you do because the contacts you make on our site will prove invaluable. We try to keep spammers off the site, but chances are they already have yours, ours, and all of our collective third cousins' e-mail addresses anyway, alas.

Next, click to indicate that you agree with our legalities of service. If you want to read those, go to the "Main Menu" (down the left side column of the main page) and follow the "Legal" and "Privacy" links).

Logging In

Once you've received your registration e-mail with its password (this should be almost instantaneous), you can now log into weekendmillionaire.com as a member (welcome!).

The "Login" block is on the top of the right side column. Type in your user name and password, and the system tells you that it's logging you in. That's all there is to it.

My Account

When you log in for the first time, you might want to check the "Main Menu" block again (down the left side column). You'll see that a new link has now appeared called "My Account." This link is only there when you are logged in.

Click on "My Account" to change items in your personal information, including changing from the weird password the system issued in its initial e-mail to one you can remember more easily.

To change your password: log in, click on "My Account," click on "Change Your Settings," and then (down at the bottom of that screen) type in your new password twice.

Lost Password

Lost your password? No problem. Click the "Log in Problems?" link in the "Login" block (top of the right side column), and then click the "Retrieve Lost Password," link and an e-mail will be sent to you. Then follow these steps:

- Retrieve your e-mail, and return to the site by *following the link in the e-mail.*
- Click "Retrieve Lost Password" again.
- Enter your user name and the confirmation code supplied in the e-mail in the appropriate box.
- Click "Send Password" again.
- You will receive a message that a new password has been generated and e-mailed to you. Get that e-mail.
- Follow the link in the e-mail back to the site, and return to the "Login" block.
- Enter your user name and new password, click "Remember Me," and then click the "Login" button.

Taking the Grand Tour

Okay, we've looked at the basics. Now let's board the bus for a quick tour of the weekendmillionaire.com site. To cover it all comprehensively would require more space than we have in this book and bus fuel is kinda expensive these days as well. But we'll hit the highlights and give you an introduction to the knowledge needed to find your way around on your own. We encourage you to visit and play with the site as much as you like—that's the way you really learn. Also, as we've told you, we keep adding features, so new things will be popping up from time to time. We guarantee it!

The main page of the site (refer again to Figure B1-2) comes up when you enter weekendmillionaire.com in the address block of your browser. Below the header information, such as the title of the site and the menu bar described in the preceding section, the page is divided into three columns— narrower ones on the left and right and the wider main column in the center where articles live. We'll look at features in the left column first.

Surveying the Left Column

The left column is on the . . . oh, you know that.

Well, how about this? Columns are divided into boxes. You might bring up the weekendmillionaire.com site and follow along, trying out each feature, as you read this section. We'll start, logically enough, with the top box in the left column.

By the way, this left column—which contains most of the important navigation links—appears on most pages. The right column usually disappears on pages other than the "Home" page to give more room for reading articles or displaying information.

Quick Menu

The top left box is the "Quick Menu." The menu selections here mostly echo the menu bar we've already met earlier.

The "Investor Clubs" link provides access to a searchable database containing contact information and meeting times/locations of real estate investment clubs all over the country. Please feel free to use the "Contact Us" link (it's in the "Main Menu" box in the left column) to let us know about any clubs we did not list or corrections to information about your club.

An additional link is for "Site Awards," showing some of the awards our Web site has garnered. The "Quick Menu" is more likely to have selections added than the menu bar (less room there). Yes, some redundancy in menu links exists here and elsewhere. Just use the link that's closest to where you are on the page. The reason for both this menu and the menu bar is convenience and flexibility and to avoid having to scroll down the page to the "Main Menu" just to find the most often accessed destinations.

Events Calendar

Next down we find the "Events Calendar." Mike and Roger speak all over the country (both individually and together), they appear at book signings, and they're interviewed on radio and television—some of which get listed in the "Events Calendar." Also, and this is important, when chats are scheduled, you'll find that notification in this box.

There's more to the "Events Calendar" than what you see in the box. If you click on a date in the calendar, all the events for that day will be shown. And there is also a search feature just for events (click on the "Search" button at the bottom of the box).

Main Menu

Under the "Events Calendar" is the "Main Menu" box. It contains a lot of links you might need only occasionally. Items such as "Home," "Contact Us,"

"Submit Feedback," "Mike Summey Bio," "Roger Dawson Bio," and "Legal" and "Privacy" policies are all pretty self-explanatory.

The "Utilities" submenu has more items, some of which are active and some of which eventually will be active or disappear. Again, this site changes.

Of these "Utilities" items, some are quite useful and/or interesting. "AvantGo," for example, supplies a version of Web site articles suitable for mobile phones that have Web browsing capabilities. If you use the AvantGo.com Web site, you can subscribe to our channel or, with a little effort, you can access us direct with your phone or personal digital assistant (PDA). We do not charge for direct access.

The "Members List" selection takes you to a page where you can search for and find other members of the site (we are into the thousands of members now, and membership continues to grow—again, it's free!).

We hope that you'll use the "Recommend Us" link to let your friends know about our site.

"Stats" shows how many visits we've had. "Search" is another very handy way to find things on the site. "Topics" lists the topics covered (just click on any topic, and it will show you all the articles relating to that topic).

Last Forum Posts

Our forums get covered in detail in Chapter B3, but this box shows the most recent posts. Clicking on any title of a post takes you to that post in the forums so that you can read it.

Roger Dawson

We put Roger in a box, and watch him dance! Roger Dawson—in addition to being coauthor of the *Weekend Millionaire* series—is the leading speaker on the profitable art of power negotiating. This box, with the small, constantly playing video of Roger in action, also gives you a link to Roger's personal Web site at rdawson.com, which uses the same software as weekendmillionaire.com.

News

The "News" box offers a handy scrolling list of articles published recently on our site. Clicking on the title of any article transports you to the article.

Newsletter Archive

Here live copies of our previous newsletters for your perusal and enjoyment. We plan on stepping up the frequency of newsletter mailings. Joining our site automatically puts you on the mailing list. Don't be concerned—you will never be required to pay anything or buy anything.

Online

Finally, in the left column, we have the "Online" box. This tells you how many guests and members are online at the moment. We love to look and see big numbers here, so visit us early and often.

Center Stage in the Center Column

The center column on the main page basically shows you articles. Clicking on the title of an article displays the full article for ease of reading. You will notice also that each article has a topic logo. For example, articles by or about Mike Summey use his photo as a logo. Clicking on the topic logo shows you *all* articles in this topic.

In Figure B1-7, we have clicked on the title of an article about Mike's new aircraft (a Beechcraft King Air). Note that the right-hand column has hidden itself to make the article easier to read.

Currently, we display the 10 most recent articles on the main page. Older stories may be accessed in several ways, including using the "Search" box, clicking on a topic logo, or though the "Past Articles" box we'll meet shortly when looking at the right column of the main page.

Getting Right with the Right Column

This column holds some handy boxes of goodies also. The most important one is at the top.

Login

The "Login" box is where members sign onto the site (see Figure B1-8). Click on "New User Signup" in the "Quick Menu" if you're not a member— it's free to join, and you get additional privileges, such as the capability to post information or questions in the forums, e-mail notifications of chats, and more to come. This box also provides a way to have your password e-mailed to you should you be a member but have forgotten your password.

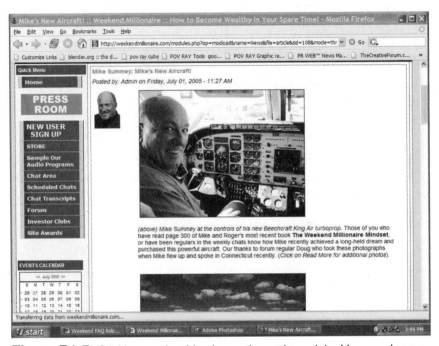

Figure B1-7 Clicking on the title shows the entire article. Here we have a short article about Mike's new aircraft.

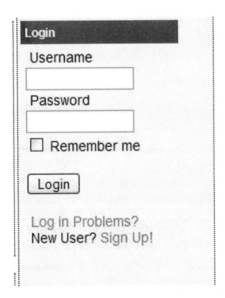

Figure B1-8 The "Login" box lets members log in.

Search

The "Login" box disappears after you sign in, making the "Search" box now the top box. In "Getting Around" earlier in this chapter we discussed what a useful tool searching is. Use it in good health, and find a lot.

The Weekend Millionaire

The "Weekend Millionaire" box shows book covers (click on them to buy from Amazon.com or click on "Store" on the menu bar at the top of the page to buy directly from us). You also can buy personalized signed bookplates to affix in your books by clicking on the link in this box, and you can get information on buying the *Weekend Millionaire* series of books in wholesale quantities.

We Recommend

Famous real estate guru and television personality Carleton Sheets is a long-time friend of Mike and Roger. In this box are links to some of Carleton's highly recommended real estate tools. We'll be adding other recommendations as we find products that we feel comfortable recommending.

Other Books & Things

This box provides links to various real estate and negotiating books and programs. Clicking on these links takes you to Amazon.com. Any purchase made from clicking on these links generates a small commission that helps to keep this site free.

Make Us Your Home on the Net!

Two buttons in this box let you find us easier. Clicking on "Set Home Page" will cause your browser to make us the home page that comes up first thing. And "Add to Favorites" puts us in your bookmarks (this works only in Internet Explorer; see Chapter B4 for other ways of making us your home page or adding weekendmillionaire.com as a bookmark).

Past Articles

As mentioned when we were looking at the center column, only the 10 most recent articles are displayed. Links to older articles can be found in this box. Also, the "Search" box or clicking on a topic logo lets you retrieve *any* article (no matter how old).

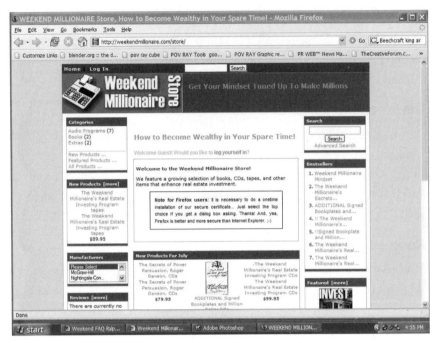

Figure B1-9 The Weekend Millionaire Store provides easy, secure shopping.

Visit Our Store

Finally, in the grand tour, we come to the "Weekend Millionaire Store" (see Figure B1.9). We offer this as a convenient way to obtain our books, audio and video programs, and other special products. Please feel free to check it out.

As You Leave the Bus

Thanks for taking the grand tour. Remember, this brief look at weekendmillionaire.com only gives you an introduction—there's a great deal more to see, learn, and enjoy. Please spend some time taking a look and experimenting with our various features. Don't worry, you can't break anything.

And remember, there are two more important areas to see, both within walking distance—the *chat* area and *forums*. Those chapters come next, along with a final chapter on some miscellaneous tidbits, including other ways to find information and how you can get help directly from us.

B2

Chats

One of weekendmillionaire.com's most popular features is our *online chats*. A "chat," of course, is a conversation, and "online" chat programs allow users—by connecting them over the Web—to converse via two-way typing in real time (live, as if you would want to converse any other way). The area where this happens is called a "chat room," and dozens or scores of people can be in it at any one time.

When to Chat

We offer two basic types of chats. First, the chat room (weekendmillionaire .com/chat) runs all the time. So check it regularly for *informal* chatting opportunities. Whenever two or more people are in the chat area, 24/7, feel free to talk about real estate investing and so forth. You'll find folks doing and learning the same things you are—making new friends all over the world and networking with fellow investors. This can be an invaluable resource for you!

The second type of chat—"formal" chats—are announced ahead of time and usually occur on Monday evenings at 8 p.m. Eastern time each week that Mike or Roger is available. We send out e-mails to members notifying you of these scheduled events. Nonmembers are also welcome, and you can find out about chats and other events by checking the "Events Calendar" box—second box down in the left column of the weekendmillionaire.com "Home" page.

These well-attended formal chats often include—in addition to Mike Summey and Roger Dawson—nationally known guests such as Carleton Sheets and Al Lowry, and other notable real estate experts, as well as real estate attorneys, bankers, insurance professionals, property managers, and tax experts who offer free advice. Watch the "Events Calendar" for details.

Finding the Chat Room

Like any good meeting place, the weekendmillionaire.com chat room has several entrances. The direct address is weekendmillionaire.com/chat (as you recall from the preceding chapter, no *www* needed in the address).

From the "Home" page of our site, you have two doors into the chat area. In the "Quick Menu" on the top upper-left column of the "Home" page (and on most other pages as well), just click on "Chat Area" (see Figure B2-1). And the "Chat" selection on the "Menu Bar" in the header area of most pages (see Figure B2-2) takes you there as well.

The weekendmillionaire.com chat software requires *Java*, a programming language for Web applications. Almost all Web browsers these days come with *Java* included. Alas, in some, it's not activated. Check the "Help" facility in your particular browser for instructions on how to get *Java* working—you'll need it lots more places on the Web in addition to our chat.

Once you click on one or the other entrance links into the chat area, a Web page comes up that initially presents you with a large gray box. Be patient, that's the *Java* "applet" (program) loading, and loading slowly initially is a characteristic of *Java* beyond our control. Therefore, depending on the type and speed of your Internet connection, it may take a few moments, but the wait is worthwhile. The gray may turn white with Sun's *Java* logo on it (Sun Microsystems is the company that publishes *Java*) if this is the

Figure B2-1 The "Chat Area" selection on the "Quick Menu" takes you to the chat room's sign-in page.

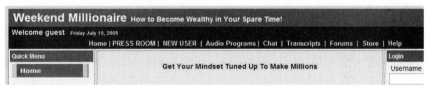

Figure B2-2 The "Chat" selection on the "Menu Bar" also takes you to the chat room's sign-in page.

first time you've accessed the page, or it might just go ahead and pop up the login page. Regardless, the login page is what you're waiting on.

Logging into the Chat

Once the chat login page appears (see Figure B2-3), type a user name in the "Username" block. Please use a short, easy-to-type name. We've made this part easy. No prior registration is required for joining our chats; enter any name you like. We suggest that you take this ongoing opportunity for gaining profitable knowledge seriously—use your real name instead of hiding

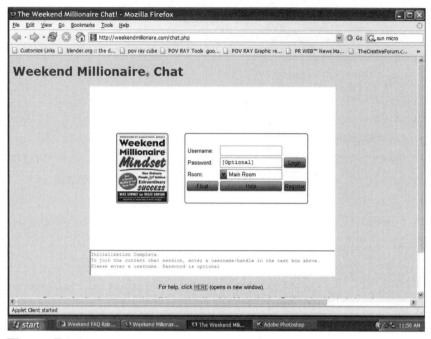

Figure B2-3 The chat login page.

behind some fanciful made-up name. This also means that we can address you as Bill or Debbie in the chat rather than the cumbersome "Future_millionaire_in_Hackensack." We're a friendly and helpful bunch.

This chat system does not allow blanks (spaces) in names. Therefore, in using your real name or any user name of two or more words, replace spaces by inserting an underscore (_) or hyphen (-) in the user name. For example, Ralph_Roberts would be a legitimate way to show a real name.

Don't worry about choosing a short name just for convenience, the chat software is smart. If you log in with your full name like Ralph_Roberts and someone types, "Hi Ralph," the system beeps on Ralph's computer to let him know he's been addressed directly. It beeps for the full name also.

If you try logging in with spaces in a user name, the following error message appears:

"Invalid Username or Password. Please try again."

Just replace spaces to fix it.

In the chat itself, your user name will look like this:

Mike_Summey: Where's Roger?

Roger must have been a little late that night, eh? But he's usually there on time. Now—on to passwords.

You'll note the term "[optional]" in the "Password" block. As stated earlier, no registration is required; hence usually the only people who need to enter a password (we cover the exception below) are "moderators." Moderators are the "bouncers" who chuck out any one abusing the privilege of the chat by being an idiot, and they have the power to ban such abusers from reentering. But don't worry—in the two years we've held regular chats, no one has ever had to be escorted to the door. We seem to attract good people. Thank you!

Quick Login

To take it down to the basics of logging in to the chat—enter your user name in the "Username" block and either click on the blue "Login" button or just hit the "Enter" key on your computer's keyboard—gently please, or you'll spill your [substitute beverage of choice here].

Getting Help

Staying on the "Login" page for a moment, there are several items below the blue "Login" button. You do not have to worry about "Room" yet because we only offer one chat room.

The blue "Float" button opens the "Login" page as a separate page in your browser. We suggest that you do not use this yet (we'll show you a better way after you're actually in the chat room itself).

Also, the blue "Register" button can be ignored because we do not require registration yet. However, if you want to lock in a particular user name so that no one else can use it, feel free. In this case you will be assigned a password and have to enter it when logging in.

Finally, the blue button that says "Help" is quite useful in refreshing your memory on how various features of the chat work. As you will see, we use the *SigmaChat* software and highly recommend it (see SigmaChat.com for more details).

Below the "Login" applet window there is another link to the same help pages, and below that we come to the legalities you agree to by entering the chat.

Legalities

Our weekly chats in large part provided the questions we answered in this book. Of course, we did answer the questions briefly as they were asked, but *reanswering* them in these pages gave us the scope to research and elaborate. We thank everyone who participated and hope that we haven't embarrassed anyone.

But just to dot the *t*'s and "cross the eyes" of the lawyers, we do call your attention to the statement at the bottom of the "Login" page:

> Transcripts from formal, pre-announced chats will be posted on this Web site following the chat. Entering and participating in these chats constitutes permission to use your questions and comments in these postings and other published materials. . . .

And we include a link so that you can read the raw transcripts for yourself.

So, yes, more books will come as we get more questions, which benefits everyone. Participate in our chats, and you get double bang or more for your buck (which you don't have to pay anyway). We answer you immediately (one bang), and we expand on the questions in later publications (several more resounding bangs). Enjoy.

Chatting

Figure B2-4 depicts the "Chat" page. It's nice but a bit small when several people are in the chat, all typing away. Most of us like to enlarge the chat area to make it easier to read and follow the thread of conversations. Do this by clicking on the "Float/Dock" button (don't ya just love computer jargon?). You'll find that this button is third from the right in the toolbar (see Figure B2-5). It has a little square superimposed over another little square, denoting making a small window larger.

The large window is called "floating" and the small window (original page) is "docked." Just think of them as large and small. See Figure B2-6 for

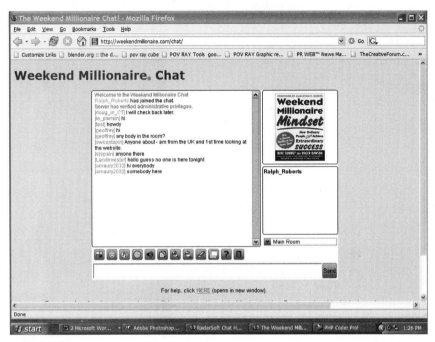

Figure B2-4 The "Chat" page.

the large window. As you can see in the figure, the chat system remembers the last few messages typed into it, even for days.

Chat Page Layout, Left and Right

The largest area by far on the "Chat" page is the message window (the large block in the left column), where you and the other chat participants' conversations appear.

On the upper right is a small advertisement area. Click on the product advertised and you'll be taken to the appropriate location where you can purchase it. Please!

Figure B2-5 The "Chat" toolbar.

Figure B2-6 The expanded, or floating, "Chat" page.

Below that, in the right column, a list shows who is in the chat room at any given time. During the popular formal chats, this list gets so long that you have to scroll up and down to see it all.

And the last little window in the right column allows you to change chat rooms. We currently have only one room operating, but if others are opened, this is where you will switch between them.

Chat Page, Bottom

Two blocks live on the bottom of the "Chat" page. The first of these (the top one) is the "toolbar" (refer again to Figure B2-5). And the bottom is where you type your part of the conversation. This is a multiline text box, so type all you want to say and press "Enter" on your keyboard to send the message. Your message will appear in the large message box in sequence with what everyone else is saying. Read it before you send it to be sure that it makes sense, but nobody is a stickler for spelling, punctuation, or grammar in chats.

Chats

If numerous people are talking at once, conversations run in "threads"—that is, with several people talking at once, the topics get intertwined and are not one line after the other. Don't worry, you'll get used to this quickly. It's like standing in a cocktail party and hearing six conversations going on around you; you'll get the gist of the various conversations pretty much instinctively, and if you are engaged in a conversation, you will quickly learn to look for replies from the person you are talking with.

Once you've typed something, others will read what you have typed and respond to you. If you wish to get someone specific's attention, just include their name at the beginning of the message that you are typing. Their message will appear in a different color, and *their* computer will beep to alert them.

Toolbar Functions

Below we list the functions of each toolbar button. Feel free to play with them whenever you find the chat room free. You'll learn these quickly, and some of them add a lot of fun to the chat experience.

We go from left to right (as shown in Figure B2-5):

- *Color button* (four small colored squares icon). This button allows you to change your current text color.
- *Emoticons button* (smiley face icon). This button allows you to select an emoticon from the emoticon popup window, and it inserts itself into your current message.
- *Audio emoticons button* (musical note icon). This button allows you to select an audio emoticon from the emoticon popup window.
- *Timestamp button* (clock icon). This button allows you to enable or disable timestamps.
- *Audio button* (small speaker icon). This button allows you to enable or disable audio within the chat room.
- *Copy content button* (two pieces of note paper icon). This button allows you to copy content from the chat room.
- *Font zoom-in button* (magnifying glass with plus symbol icon). This button allows you to increase the current font size.
- *Font zoom-out button* (magnifying glass with minus symbol). This button allows you to decrease the current font size.

- *Clear screen* (eraser icon). This button allows you to clear the contents of the chat screen.
- *Float/dock button* (two little windows icon). This button allows you to float or dock the chat room.
- *Help button* (question mark icon). This button allows you access to the chat room help file.
- *Logout button* (exit door icon). This button will log you out of the chat room.

The "Help" button takes you to SigmaChat's (our chat software provider) "Help" page, as described earlier.

That's it. This is a fun and easy chat to use. Jump in with us! Just keep an eye on the "Events Calendar" on the weekendmillionaire.com "Home" page so that you'll know when the formal chats are scheduled, or register as a "New User," and you will receive our e-mail notices about the chats.

Chat Etiquette

In closing—let's have a word about etiquette.

Think of our live chats as having the same form and structure as a seminar in a hotel meeting room somewhere. The same rules of politeness apply.

It's okay to talk like crazy when there's no speaker, but when someone has the floor—such as Mike or Roger or one of our guests—give them the lead. They usually will accept questions, but let's not everyone jump in at once. In fact, as you can see by this book, we *want* your questions.

And finally, just be tolerant of others and do not hurt anyone's feelings. If you're an old pro, help the new beginners rather than intimidating them. If you're a new beginner, just remember that it's better to feel silly for a moment than to stay dumb the rest of your life because you're afraid to ask about something you don't understand.

So . . . see you in the next chat!

B3

Forums

At weekendmillionaire.com we offer two exciting and informative ways to interact directly with Mike Summey, Roger Dawson, other well-known real estate and investment gurus, and your friendly fellow investors. The first of these, *chats*, we've already . . . er . . . chatted about in the preceding chapter. The second you'll find are our *forums*.

What's the difference? Here's an analogy: You're walking down the street and see Sam. You and Sam stop, find a nice spot in the shade (it's summer), and begin discussing the best rental properties. Bill comes along and sees you two and joins in. This is a live conversation with questions and answers in real time. It's a "chat"—just as when you're in weekendmillionaire.com's chat area, typing your conversations back and forth, also in real time.

Now the "forums" (we use the word in its plural form because the "Forums" area is divided into several topics) is more like a bulletin board: Sam comes along, finds a couple of unused thumbtacks, and pins up (we call it "posting") a question on rental properties. You happen along after work on your way home and read Sam's note. You tack up an answer beneath Sam's. Bill can't sleep two nights later and is up at two in the morning, comes by, and tacks up a helpful elaboration on your answer, as do Mike and Roger when they get a few minutes.

Both types of interactive communications have their place, and both enhance and expand the investing knowledge you gain through the *Weekend Millionaire* series of books and audio programs. And even more important—since both chats and forums are interactive—you can tailor your online experience at weekendmillionaire.com to answer questions you specifically have.

The weekendmillionaire.com forum system runs on highly popular standard bulletin board software (specifically *phpBB* in this case). Most likely you've already used such forums on other sites and already can find your way around easily, but here are the basics of how to use our forums.

Finding the Forums Area

Getting to the "Forums" area is easy (see Figure B3-1). Just click on the "Forums" selection in the "Quick Menu" at the top of the left column on the "Home" page or on the same word on the black menu bar across the top of most pages.

Like Harry Potter riding a broom, you fly right to the forums.

Membership

Anyone, even an anonymous guest, can read the messages posted in the "Forums." *However*, membership (did we mention that it's free?) in weekendmillionaire.com is required to post replies or to start new "threads" (subjects) of conversation.

The membership requirement for posting became necessary because of abuses from spammers. Keeping our topics on topic with interesting and informative posts about real estate investing is always our goal.

Walking Among the Forums

The "Forums" at weekendmillionaire.com currently fall into eight *topic areas* (see Figure B3-2). Each topic area contains *topics threads,* or mes-

Figure B3-1 Clicking on "Forums" on the "Quick Menu" or on the menu bar takes you to the "Forums" area.

sages, posted on a specific subject. It is common courtesy (which the forum moderators enforce) to *stay on topic*—that is, post messages in a topic thread only concerning what the thread is about. This makes it easy for everyone interested in answers to specific questions to find those answers.

Topics

Following are our current topic areas—but we'll add more as we think of them or receive requests from you and other folks frequenting the forums as to what you'd find useful.

Getting Real Estate Information 24/7

Figure B3-2 The main "Forums" index shows all the topic areas.

- *News*—for information pertaining to this site and its related products; this area allows only moderators to post, all other areas allow any registered member to post.
- *The Weekend Millionaire*—for discussions about the *Weekend Millionaire* series of books by Mike Summey and Roger Dawson.
- *Computerized Real Estate*—a place to discuss real estate and investing software packages.
- *Internet and Web*—great sites you've found in browsing for investments.

Forums

- *Investing*—general discussions about investing in real estate.
- *Mike Summey*—Mike's forum.
- *Roger Dawson*—Roger's forum.
- *Government and Such*—a place for friendly debate about taxes and other governmental actions concerning the real estate investor.

Reading Topic Areas

To read a forum, you have two choices: Click on its title, and all the subtopics in that forum (we'll use "The Weekend Millionaire" as an example) are displayed on a separate page. Or since these subtopics also show on the main "Forums" index page (see Figure B3-2), just click on the subtopic you want. We'll look at "Books." Click on it if you're following along on the Web site and you see a screen very like Figure B3-3.

We call the list of message subjects that now shows "conversation threads." These are questions, answers, and observations relating to that

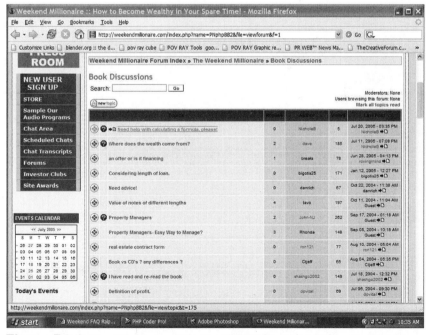

Figure B3-3 The "Books" subtopic of "The Weekend Millionaire" topic area.

subject. And again, it is good etiquette to stay on topic (post only about the current subject within that thread) so that answers are easier to find without wading through a bunch of extraneous verbiage.

Figure B3-4 shows an example of a posted message. After reading a message, you have several options. The first, of course, is just to continue on to the next message posted or to go back and choose another thread or topic. But let's look at the buttons just below the message itself. You have several choices, which we'll detail in a moment, and two more if you are the one who posted the message originally.

In this latter case (you're the poster), a small "x" button is over on the right. Click that if you want to delete your message. Naturally, you cannot delete anyone else's posting unless you have administrative privileges. There is also an "Edit" button—which allows you to edit your posting to fix typos or correct other mistakes.

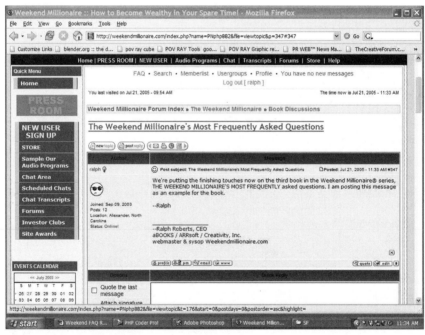

Figure B3-4 Example of a posted message.

The four buttons on the left perform these functions:

- *Profile.* Clicking here shows you information about the poster (this is drawn from whatever you've entered about yourself when you joined *weekendmillionaire.com*).
- *Pm.* Send the poster a "private message." Private messages are not e-mail but messages that appear only to the recipient the next time he or she logs onto the site.
- *E-mail.* Send the poster a conventional e-mail.
- *WWW.* If the poster has listed a personal Web site in his or her personal profile, this gives you a link to it.

Now the buttons on the right (and only two appear unless this is a message you posted, in which case there also will be an "Edit" button) are

- *Quote.* Pressing the "Quote" button brings up a reply page and inserts the message text you've been reading into it as a quote. It is common sense to quote the message you are replying to or asking about to avoid confusion when there are lots of other messages in the thread.
- *Up Arrow.* Takes you back to the top of the page.

Posting

"Posting" simply means replying to a message. Several ways exist to do this. You can click on the "Quote" button in the message (as we saw earlier), or you can type in the "Quick Reply" box or click on the "Post Reply" button beneath that box for a page with more options than "Quick Reply" offers. There is also a "New Topic" button. Use this if you want to post a comment that falls within the general topic area but is out of this particular conversation thread. Figure B3-5 illustrates the message posting page with its additional options.

The full reply page offers options such as Hypertext Markup Language (HTML), the basic underlying format of the Web. If you know such things as "<I>" starts italics and "</I>" ends italics, you can do that to spice up the appearance of your messages. You also can add links and photos. Showing you how is beyond the scope of this book; that's just general Web knowledge available in all sorts of places. Enjoy!

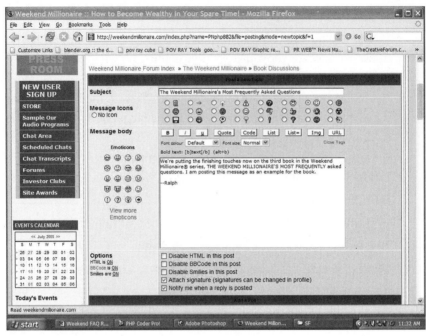

Figure B3-5 Full message posting page.

Emoticons

"Emoticons" are all those little smiley faces, etc. Feel free to use them in making your posts more expressive. It's okay to have fun while soaking up all the many tips on real estate investing you'll find in our forums.

Referring to Figure B3-5 again, you'll see that there are two blocks of emoticons. The block on the top lets you put an emoticon in your subject title. The block on the left inserts emoticons into the text of your message.

Like, have fun, dude.

Additional Help

This chapter, owing to a lack of space, covers only the basic usage of our forums. The best way to get additional help these days is through *your* computer. Go back to the main index or starting page of the weekendmillionaire. com forums. Look for the "FAQ" link along the top of the "Forums" window.

Forums

By this time, having read this book and noted its title, you know that "FAQ" means "frequently asked questions." It's one of those all-pervasive Internet acronyms that have been around for decades before the Web itself (The Internet has been here since the late sixties, but the Web only came into being in 1991).

The forums FAQ will answer many of your specific questions, and you also can always Google (or use some other Web search service) for more general examples of how forums work.

The weekendmillionaire.com forums are an exceptionally excellent and even entertaining way of interacting with your fellow investors and learning more about how you can start building wealth for yourself. Please take advantage of our offerings in this area—yes, it's still *free*.

B4

Other Sources of Information

Yep, weekendmillionaire.com (again, you can forget about the *www;* it's not necessary)—as explained in the first chapter of this Bonus Section—is a *dynamic* Web site generating literally *thousands* of pages depending on your input. Our site serves as your ongoing *interactive* mentor for the Weekend Millionaire concept of real estate investment and wealth building—a concept that has been proven over 30 years not just by Mike and Roger but by numerous others who have benefited from advice freely given through books, audio programs, and hundreds of seminars and other speaking engagements.

This chapter shows you easy ways of finding weekendmillionaire.com and, as a bonus, additional information on *millions* of other real estate–related sites.

Make Us Your Home on the Web

Since you've gotten this far, we assume that you find our concept interesting and weekendmillionaire.com a useful tool in learning more about it on a continuing basis. May we suggest that you bookmark the site for convenience in finding and returning for regular visits or even select us as your "home page" (the page your browser shows every time you start it up).

A "browser" is a computer program that lets you surf Web pages. On the majority of computers it's Microsoft's *Internet Explorer* (little blue script *e* icon). On Apple Macintosh computers it's often *Safari*. Other browsing software include *Opera* (very fast) and the fast-growing in numbers *Firefox*.

Firefox's popularity derives from its enhanced security over *Internet Explorer* (although the newly announced *Internet Explorer 7* supposedly narrows the gap). At any one time these days, hundreds of computer criminals simultaneously try to break into millions of computers, turn them into "zombies" (controlling your computer without your knowledge), and (often) use them to send out streams of spam e-mails. As a Web master, stopping these idiots from using my servers is a constant fight, but it's your fight as well—all of us—so that we can keep our wonderful and indispensable Internet usable. Make sure that you have antivirus and firewall protection on your PC, and use a secure browser.

Internet Explorer

If you still use *Internet Explorer*, we make things easy for you. On the weekendmillionaire.com "Home" page, go down the right-hand column until you find the block labeled "Make Us Your Home on the Net!" (see Figure B4-1).

There are two buttons in this block—"Set Home Page" and "Add to Favorites." "Set Home Page" (the biggest change) makes weekendmillionaire.com the home page your browser goes to when it first opens or when you click on the little house/home icon at the top of the browser screen. The bottom button, "Add to Favorites," is less intrusive—this simply adds weekendmillionaire.com to your browser's bookmarks. *Internet Explorer* calls bookmarks "Favorites," and you access them by clicking on that word at the top of your browser screen.

Figure B4-1 Use *Internet Explorer* as your browser? We make finding us again easy!

Manually Entering Home Page and Bookmarks

Now—if you have *Firefox* or most other browsers—security features usually require you perform these operations manually, that is, making a Web page your home page or entering a bookmark.

Using *Firefox* as an example, first go to weekendmillionaire.com. On the top menu line of your browser, click on "Tools," and then (on the next screen) click on "Options." You should now have the "Options" dialog box (see Figure B4-2). Click on the "Use Current Page" button. The full link to us, http://weekendmillionaire.com, appears in the small box above the button. Click "OK" at the bottom of the "Options" dialog box, and you are done. From now on, weekendmillionaire.com will be your home page that shows each time the browser is activated or where you go after clicking on the little house/home icon.

You may, of course, simply wish to bookmark us instead of making weekendmillionaire.com your home page. That's fine, too—and even easier. Simply go to weekendmillionaire.com, hold down your "Ctrl" key, and tap the "D" key once. This brings up the small dialog box shown in Figure B4-3.

Click on "OK," and it's done. Access your bookmark by clicking on "Bookmarks" at the top of your browser screen and then clicking on the link

Figure B4-2 Setting the "Home" page in *Firefox* is done in the "Options" dialog box.

name (that's what shows in the "Name" box in Figure B4-3 when the book-mark is created). You also may like to bookmark other pages on our site that you return to often, such as "Chat," "Forums," and so forth.

Finding *Lots* More Information

Let's not stop finding other sources. Yes, weekendmillionaire.com gives you thousands of pages, but right there on your desktop, the kitchen table, or

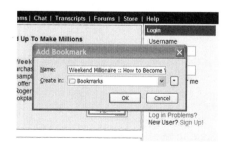

Figure B4-3 Setting a bookmark in *Firefox* is done in the "Options" dialog box.

wherever, you have the world's *largest* real estate and wealth-building library—your PC hooked up to the Internet. Literally millions upon millions of highly useful pages are there for your almost instant access. The only problem is *finding them* amid billions of pages of junk (and some really *interesting* stuff, too, but it won't make you wealthy).

Many, many ways exist to search the Web and narrow that search down to a manageable list of results. These facilities are called "search engines." You type in a term of something you want to find out more about—such as "real estate"—and you get links to pages that contain your search term. You'll get flooded with them, actually, if you don't know how to search effectively.

We'll give you some brief tips on using one of the more common, popular methods of searching, google.com (no *www* necessary there either).

Type "google.com" in the address line box at the top of your browser and hit the "Enter" key on your keyboard. You'll get a screen containing the information in Figure B4-4.

Now, let's look at a quick example that will get you started searching and mining productive results from the otherwise intimidating deluge of data. Say that you want to check out houses for sale in Asheville, North Carolina, up in the Blue Ridge Mountains—the "Land of the Sky." Mike and Ralph both live near Asheville. Roger, he hangs his hat in California.

- Business Solutions - About Google

©2005 Google - Searching 8,168,684,336 web pages

Figure B4-4 The Google search engine start screen.

In the "Search" box on google.com, you could type "houses for sale" as the search term. Try it. I get over eight million results. Ummm, takes a while to check all those out, but I'm sure some of those houses will be in Asheville.

Time for narrowing down the results. Therefore, next, we'll use a very useful trick, the hyphen (-) character. Using the search term "houses-for-sale" tells Google that you want only pages that have those three words adjacent. Try that. Ah! Better. Only 768,000. Of course, they are spread all over the world.

More honing of our search. Type in "houses-for-sale Asheville" (upper-case or lowercase, it does not matter). Hmmm. Even better. Only about 24,500 results, but still more than you can check before supper. Continue adding terms to get fewer and fewer results (but more appropriate to your area of interest). For example, "houses-for-sale Asheville Sunset-Mountain" gives you only 110 results for a section of the city boasting more luxurious homes than the norm.

And that's the basic technique. Just come up with search terms that eliminate all those billions of other sites.

Google, by the way, has some other really neat features. Play with google.com/maps. You can plan trips, look at the locations of houses you might want to purchase (see if schools, churches, malls, and so forth are nearby), even see photos of them from space! For example, Figure B4-5 shows Roger's office in Placentia, California (wave at us, Roger).

Practice effectively searching the Web with Google and other search engines. You'll find an endless source of profitable, appropriate, and interesting information.

Contacting Us

In earlier chapters—as well as in this one—we've mentioned several other ways of getting information. One of the best is simply to join weekendmillionaire.com, which puts you on the mailing list for announcements and for our occasional newsletter mailings. You also can ask questions by using the "Contact Us" link on the "Main Menu" (go down the left column of the "Home" page, and you'll see it).

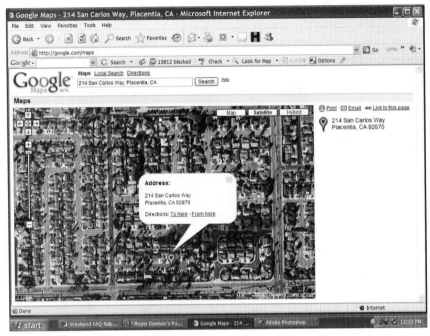

Figure B4-5 Roger's office from space.

And of course, you may contact us directly via e-mail, and time permitting, we'll reply. Our e-mail addresses are

- Mike Summey (real estate investing and the *Weekend Millionaire Mindset*)—mike@weekendmillionaire.com
- Roger Dawson (real estate investing and power negotiation)—roger@weekendmillionaire.com
- Ralph Roberts (anything about the Web site)—ralph@weekend-millionaire.com

Finally, we want to express our sincere gratitude to our great publisher, McGraw-Hill Trade, for its support in maintaining this Web site for our readers.

Index

Index

Index

Greenspan, Alan, 132
Gross leases, 191
Gross rent multiplier, 32

Handy person, 39, 199–200
HELOC (*see* Home-equity line of
    credit [HELOC])
"Higher authority" gambit, 111,
    118, 120
Home-equity line of credit
    (HELOC):
    assumable, 80–81
    credit scores and, 155–156
    home-equity loan versus, 81
    for investment properties, 7,
        13, 19–20, 22, 137–138
Homeowners' associations,
    181

Imputed interest, 81–82
Income-to-value relationship,
    22–23
Inflation, 5, 10, 27, 207
Inherited property, 66–67,
    105–106
Inspections, 49, 86, 162
Insurance:
    mortgage, 149
    payments for, 39
    on properties, 158
    title, 71, 93, 161–162, 197
Interest-only loans, 132–133,
    138, 157, 164

Interest rates:
    impact of, 5–6, 61
    imputed interest and,
        81–82
    owner financing and, 160
Internal Revenue Service
    (IRS):
    direct principal reduction
        loans and, 82
    trust deeds and, 80
Internet:
    car negotiations and, 127
    DBA (doing business as)
        searches, 118–119
    financial calculators and, 78,
        164
    market research on, 44,
        254–255
    public records and, 161
    (*See also*
        Weekendmillionaire.com)
Internet Explorer,
    251–252
Investment properties (*see*
    Multifamily properties)
Isaac, Earl, 155–156

Land:
    as investment, 96–97, 99
    trailer parks, 52, 190
Lead paint liability, 49
Lease options, 15, 16–17, 51,
    86, 134, 211
Lee, Al, 132

Index

Index

Index

Index

Index

Index